HOLDING WATER

You Truly Never Know a Woman

FELICIA R. WILSON

Scripture quotations are taken from the Holy Bible, New Living Translation, copyright ©1996, 2004, 2015 by Tyndale House Foundation. Used by permission of Tyndale House Publishers, Carol Stream, Illinois 60188. All rights reserved.

Book Design by Allison Denise of Brand It Beautifully™

ISBN: 978-0-578-97101-8

Printed in the United States of America

TABLE OF CONTENTS

Dedication vi

Acknowledgements vii

Prologue xi

I Am The City 1

Be Well, Not In The Well 11

Jasmine, Chike, & Ife 19

Sunflower Child 39

Not Broken, Just Broke 65

The Dog & The God 95

Rooted 137

Cross The River 157

Broken Mirror 179

Ebb & Flow 197

Aphule 203

Rivers 211

About The Author 219

DEDICATION

THIS BOOK IS dedicated to anyone struggling to heal what is broken in their lives. Allow your pain to become your greatest asset. Women, be willing to heal the broken girl inside; men be willing to heal the broken boy inside. To my ancestors who I have come to know and appreciate: thank you for your wisdom, insight and for helping me to understand the importance of RIVERS and MIRRORS.

This is for the bloodline of my ancestors. The Malones, Wilkes, Wilson, Perry, Strange and Twheat. We are no longer bound by generational secrets, curses, and embarrassments. We are stronger because of the path you created to dream and aspire to be different. Because of you, I can create something different, something everlasting. From old to new, I will discover new lineage by breaking every chain negatively rooted in my blood. It starts today, right here and right now. I claim FREEDOM and move in FORMATION.

ACKNOWLEDGEMENTS

FIRST AND FOREMOST, I would like to thank GOD from whom all my blessings flow. Without You I am nothing. I am grateful that You have chosen me to walk this path called life. Over the past two years You have spoken to me by answering all my prayers. From finding ancestors, learning about cousins, and reuniting me with them; all the while giving me the ability to understand Whose I am and who I come from. From this moment forward, I will be the one to break generational curses and create a new lineage of change, starting with myself and then my children. God, please continue to use me as a vessel to do Your work and walk the path You set out for my life.

Leshaun Moore, I love you endlessly. Thank you for being the big sister I need. From our Department of Juvenile Justice days to now. I remember the day I returned to work, and you told me that I was pregnant with your nephew Jeremiah. Your motherly instinct just knew without me saying a word. Know that I appreciate your realness and rawness in every form. You are a real one, sis.

Jasmine Demps, whew!!!! Sis we made it. From broken little girls to grown women. Remember the day we spoke about our dreams and aspirations? You wanted to become a nurse and I wanted to be a criminal lawyer. Well, little did we now, God had other plans and I thank you so much for embarking on this journey with me. To see you in a place of happiness melts my heart. You are the most giving person I know and have come to appreciate. You've been my day one. I know I can count on you to ride any wave with me good or bad. Thank you for over 23 years of sisterhood. I pray that you continue to shine your bright light and pray the desires of your heart are fulfilled.

Leah Daniels, thank you for listening, understanding, and nurturing my heart. When in doubt, you helped me level up to my own expectations and challenge myself. You demonstrate what it means to defy the odds on so many levels. You were built to break the mold and I am glad to be a part of the journey with you. Now let us do it together. Changing one life at a time and creating IMPACT and leaving a legacy like no other.

Kelly Hunter; what more can I say? Thank you for teaching me about MONEY and how to make it work for me, not control me. Money mapping has become that much easier to understand and I am now able to make better financial decisions. When I asked you to join me in educating foster parents and steering young people to take the wheel to what they want success to look like you understood my plan and purpose behind my vision. Now we get to do this work together, and it feels good to be educated and to educate others about money from so many different angles. DO YOUR THANG SIS!!!!!!

Carmen Fletcher, thank you so much for seeing my vision. You have helped me through this process to laugh, love and truly understand what real forgiveness looks like in physical form. I know that my ancestors are in heaven laughing their hearts out. I pray that all your hard work comes to fruition as GOD has promised. You're doing the work chica and I am proud to have you with me on this journey riding the waves. Thank you!!!!!!!

To my love, Mathews. Thank you for your patience and ongoing support. Thank you for giving me the time needed to work on my gifts that help to nurture my talents. You are such an amazing father to our two sons, Malachi and Jeremiah. Continue to be the best man, partner, and father you are. Lastly, thank you for everything you do for me and your sons.

HOLDING WATER // FELICIA R. WILSON

PROLOGUE

THE SUN BEGAN to set on a shack that belonged to two elderly sharecroppers. The wife washed dishes in the kitchen humming *At Last* by Etta James. Her sultry echoing hum awakened the husband in a daze in their humble bed. He got up and stumbled through the rickety shack walking through the sunlit cracks in the floor, following the melody into the kitchen where he saw a strangely illuminated cord attached to his wife's back. The cord draped down her yellow dress around the wall separating the kitchen and living room and out of the door. The wife calmly dried the dishes as the sun peeked through the window and cascaded over her lightly bronzed skin as she turned and said with a smile,

"Bout time you showed up Bobby."

"Etta? Etta baby, what's going on? Why are we here?" Bobby stuttered

"We're home. What do you mean?" Etta asked.

Bobby became frustrated and shouted, "No, our home is in New York City! Why are we back here? And what's this business coming out of your back? This is a dream. I need to stop drinking."

Etta smiled and gracefully walked her husband into the next room and sat on the couch with the illuminated cord snuggled around her ankle and draping over the side of the couch. She opened a photo album and showed him photographs from their life together. They laughed as they reminisced well into the evening. As the evening drew near and the crickets and frogs went into a concert, the old man walked out to the porch. He noticed an orb of light moving towards him. He squinted to see; he thought the orb was a trick of the last bit of sunlight reflecting on wet leaves from recent rain. But the light got brighter and expanded as it inched closer.

"Etta! Etta! Come out here! Something coming!" Bobby yelled.

Etta clasped on to his hand and stood calmly with him as the cantaloupe-sized light finally arrived in front of them. A wispy, calm voice came from the orb and said,

"It is time for you to join us."

"Oh Jesus! It's aliens!" Bobby exclaimed, "You get on now we ain't going with you. Baby say a prayer! Get the oil!"

Etta chuckled and rubbed Bobby's arm and said, "Bobby, we're dead. Relax."

The orb released a rainbow wave of colors in pink, blue, light blue, purple, and red until the couple was surrounded by a dome of bright light and a fog of shifting colors. Etta stepped away from her husband as he fumbled to grab her hand back. She faced him, opened her arms and the cord attached to her back flashed a bright white light and suddenly shadows of people were standing behind her. Her body transformed from her elderly self and she became young again. Trickles of twinkling light rose up Bobby's legs and overtook his body changing him from an elderly man to his younger self. He trembled and yelped,

"Etta! Etta what is going on? Is this heaven? Hell? The half-way place? Talk to me!"

Etta was silent as a mutually robust and serenading voice took over the space and said, "We are love. We are power. We are God. You are ascended. We are Chike. We are Ife. You will become a part of us when you cleanse."

Etta smiled at her fearful husband and whispered, "Bobby, welcome home."

HOLDING WATER // FELICIA R. WILSON

I AM THE CITY

I WISH PEOPLE would take the time to look at their surroundings. New York City is an oxymoronic place to live. People walk past all these buildings created to stand among whatever gods may be. They glaze over vibrant festivals that can shake the earth. They'll peek at, but ignore street art that are our hieroglyphics of generations past, present, and to come. All of this life and people walk past it as if it were already dead; as if I were already dead.

I wish they could've seen a 21-year-old woman with teenage angst quivering as the thought of great possibilities battled with my current reality of being a foster kid aging out of the system. I sat in a chair in the Brooklyn child welfare office in front of the housing coordinator who robotically said,

"Felicia? Right?"

I nodded. And without gentle instruction or encouragement, she sat me at a table to fill out the housing package and walked away. This was supposed to help me determine where I was going to live after being in sixty-three homes in which the state deemed acceptable for a young black girl to lose herself. It didn't have to be this way. But when a mother is on heroin and the drunken father chucks a beer bottle at a four-year-old rendering them unconscious the state says we can parent this child better. It didn't help that both parents died, and I could never reunite with a healthier version of themselves.

It seemed like not one set of eyes in all those homes could see me or help me to discover myself. They could only see the brokenness that had become so familiar like the towering buildings. I was never the art on the wall that foretold greatness birthed from a troubled past. And no one paid attention when my screams for help shook the earth. So, when that woman walked away and joined other social workers laughing off their life grievances in the background, while others passed me by, not looking over or offering a helping hand, I realized I was as alone as the city.

Every time I tried to pick up the pen my hand shook. Who would have thought that I was scared; especially since I always presented myself to be so tough? It's funny what comforting methods you resort to when you're terrified. I stared at the packet, picked up the pen and my surroundings deafened and blacked out. In my mind, it was just me, the papers, my tears, and my thoughts. I began to tap my toes at a steady beat and hum track songs like the ancestors did as they built the railroad for the country's prosperity and not their own.

The life that I've known
Tap tap tap
is coming to an end
Tap tap tap
I don't know how to run a new life
I wish someone could've tucked me in,
Tap tap tap
Saying baby when you're grown
You won't be alone
Instead of getting the hell out of the way
We no longer benefit from your charitable face.
Tap tap tap

HOLDING WATER // FELICIA R. WILSON

I tapped and tapped and hummed my frustrations and fears to the annoyance of people passing me by. *Well, that got their attention finally.* Although I was scared, I knew I had no choice but to accept the unchangeable reality; I was alone. I handed in my papers and strutted out of the building mustering the courage to face this new world. As I marched through downtown Brooklyn on a brisk fall day, shuttering at my own shadow, a drunk man on the corner was singing and dancing in his tattered rags. As he spun doing his own crackhead version of the electric slide, he stepped in front of me and sang:

"If you wanna be strong, challenge a dog. If you wanna be invincible, challenge a god. Challenge your god! You ain't no dog you a god, you a god!"

He carried on singing and dancing down the street. As strange as it sounds, I felt that was God speaking to me. Pastor always says that God will reach you where you are. Until that moment, God was a concept to me. All I heard growing up was *read your bible and go to church like a good little girl and the Holy Spirit will be within you! One day you're gonna have testimony!* Well, I read the book and there I was still in the test I suppose because I found no God in me. After years of fighting through for someone to see me I realized that I didn't know myself at all. All I knew was that I was a survivor. It wasn't time for that anymore, it was time to live. I tilted my head to the sky and prayed an enraged silent prayer,

"It's all or nothing now. It's 2005 I am right here! You want me to trust in You? Come on wit it! You want this soul? You're going to have to prove to me that You're worthy of my trust."

With that my angst was lifted and I strutted through downtown Brooklyn headed to the A-Train, walking to the melody over the hard beat that is NYC traffic in the background. It became my soundtrack as my courage continued to build up while I replayed the movie that had been my life. The bottle hitting my head, my mother's death, my 62 homes that could not see me and gratitude for the one that finally did. I scurried down the steps for the A-train and stood the whole way as people continued to pass me by. Then it hit me. The reason my life was set up to fail is that there was something in my bloodline that started long before I was born. It had to be. It was a habit for them, but a curse for me. Damn.

Black women carry a blessed burden of being the carriers of the bloodline. The bloodline had survived generations of multi-faceted persecution, building a stronger generation; and then... crack and heroin. Then there was me, daughter of a drug addict, foster kid, mental trauma, health issues, trust issues, faith issues and all the ambition in the world. What could I possibly do to revoke the permission of a curse to continue? With everything that was flowing through my veins what would allow me to do that?

I got off the train and began walking to my former and final foster home on Beach Ave. in Queens. My former foster mother, Josephine, allowed me to stay there as long as I went to school and worked. Josephine is what I called her in my head. She took in whomever she could, just like Josephine Baker. Even though my time was running out to be in the house at least I had a place to lay my head down tonight. She was the only one to see me.

Beach Ave. was a mix of city, beach town, and New Jersey. The shoreline was on the right that the thug life seagulls and blackbirds patrolled. The homes and apartments with working families were on the left. They had their own personal sitcoms and soap operas performing live in front of the Avenue audience. Then there was me in the middle walking on smooth pavement and over the occasional pothole. It was...odd. But it was home, for now.

I walked down the narrow street zig-zagging my steps in a stoic silence trying to settle my hype from signing my 'release' papers. In a trance, I breezed through the front door, jogged up the stairs to my room and laid down. Staring at the ceiling, frozen in a mental space between courage and terror. I thought, "How was my black ass going to break a generational curse. Or was there even a curse? Was it just my bad luck?"

If you are serious about something, it is best to put it in writing. That is how I got to this point. Someone put my name on a paper, and I became a case number, not Felicia. Through the years I journaled and today was no different. I needed to acknowledge my feelings about my past. I had to give them a sense of belonging in a new phase of my life so I could use them to create escape routes from the root of my *curse*. They needed to envelop me and choke off my need to be tough. They needed to stop me from breathing the air of rage I had become accustomed to. They needed to cover me completely and allow me to see a light from underneath a surface of solitude.

They needed me to drown.

After writing a novel's worth of emotions over the years I decided to go back and read them. The block was unusually silent. I stared at all my feelings exposed on paper and a mural started to form from the dried ink of my story. I spun around in my chair. I could see my whole life spray-painted on every wall of my room. It was a collage of a city block of disappointment and dreams from the families I had known, opportunities unachieved, and everything I was striving for. At the center of it all was a dead sunflower emerging from concrete; it broke through but was completely destroyed from the effort.

I stared at these hieroglyphics and felt like I was unable to breathe. I screamed and cried. I was crying like the women who, like clockwork every service, would praise and run around the church with tears in their eyes. Except I didn't have the strength to jump around, all there was to do was succumb to the tears and the weight they put on my shoulders making me bend down to my knees. As my tears began to dry the mural I imagined disappeared around me, all of it except the sunflower. It stayed there like it was waiting for me to acknowledge it, but I didn't know what to do to make it bloom again.

In the past there was no controlling my situation. Through the conditioning of consistent tragedy, I had become acquainted to unchangeable situations in my life. It hardened me.

The dead sunflower would not go away. Then my pastor's last sermon crossed my mind: a time to plant and a time to uproot. You can't grow in infertile spaces so you must uproot and plant where you can grow. I could only grow if I became the author of the rest of my own story.

~

Aight, so boom. If I was going to be the author of this new story, I needed to reach back and see what really ran in my veins.

I could not just be the descendant of a junkie; there was a story before then. There had to be. Or so I hoped. As a child, I was curious about why no one came to claim me or my siblings before we were placed in foster care. Were we really that much of a disgrace? At this point it was irrelevant; I just needed to figure out who I was, and from whom I came.

The following week I submitted a DNA kit to help me find some family members. The whole process was nerve-wracking, and my thoughts got wild over the next few weeks. *What if they don't like me? What if my daddy was actually a millionaire and hid us from his rich family?.*

Finally, the email came with my results. I shook like I did the day I signed my housing papers, afraid of what it might reveal. Was it worth it to know? Should I just let it be? No, I wanted to know what it felt like to call someone cousin, auntie, uncle, grandma, grandpa. I logged in.

I started bouncing in my chair with anticipation. My Wi-Fi was operating more like dial up, loading the webpage like it was 1995. Then there they were. There was a full list of cousins, aunts, uncles, and my grandparents! There was history! There was honor! There was evidence of love and more flowing through my veins than the past that made me. All I had to do was have the courage to dig deeper and maybe one day reach out.

My eyes were glued to the computer screen like an old cartoon as I scrolled through links. I found cousins to contact and get more information on the family. But I was missing one key, my mother's birth and death certificates. I sifted through the vital records and as soon as I plugged in her information the truth of the bloodline was revealed.

I found my grandparents, Robert and Rosetta. They had passed on unfortunately. My grandmother died young from cancer and my grandfather died when I was a baby. But as I dug deeper, I saw that Robert was in the Navy, became a sharecropper, married Rosetta and they took a chance by moving to New York City for a better life. They had four children including my mother, Beverly.

I got a notification from a cousin that wanted to connect with me - C. Levinia Moore - so I eagerly clicked it and saw a very welcoming message...but no photo. We shared the eagerness to connect and chatted about how life had been going overall, like we were old friends catching up. I finally asked her how we were connected. Levinia said that we share the same great-grandparents and that they had nine children and her grandmother was one of them. Even though she was a somewhat close relative, I was curious enough to see if she knew anything about my grandparents or Beverly.

Felicia: I got put into foster care after the age of four. I found out my mother, Beverly, died on Halloween, 1988. Do you by chance know anything about my mother or grandparents?

C. Levinia: Yes. I do.

Felicia: OMG what do you know about them?!

C. Levinia: After your grandmother died, your Mom was so grief-stricken that she started using drugs. She was only 17 and didn't know how to handle that. So, it handled her. I am so sorry. Someone gave it to her to cope and she just got progressively worse.

Felicia: It's ok. At least I know now.

C. Levinia: I have to go. But I'm so glad I finally found you. There are a lot of people who have been looking for you. We'll be in touch.

She signed off after that and my soul was ignited to know that I was not forgotten, I was not alone, I was unfound. Choosing to heal was the beginning of respecting the process of getting to know me. Now I had to uncover the secrets I hid behind my smile. The smile so many walked past, just as they do the god-sized skyscrapers. I had to destroy the roots of this curse by making the pain loud enough to shake the earth. I had to paint the rest of the mural on the wall that would tell my story for more generations to heal. I am the city, and I am alive.

HOLDING WATER // FELICIA R. WILSON

BE WELL, NOT IN THE WELL

~~~~~~. ~~~~

I WALKED THROUGH a valley where I was myself, but myself was not me. Kept going until I approached a well along a line of dead trees. I shouldn't have looked in the well, but my caution was smothered by curiosity. Down there I saw a woman - frail, covered in mud, and enraged. She scraped at the sides of the stone-sealed well and screamed like she was in a cage. Scared for my life I ran, but myself that wasn't myself, said to return. I went back to the well, looked closely behind what appeared to be a monster. Low and behold it was her.

"Mama!" I cried out reaching for her weakened hand, hoping she would care enough to be strong and bring herself to dry land. She crept her way to the top and grabbed onto my eager reach. Then instead of climbing she tried to pull me down with her in the well, where her paramour, heroin, held her in hell. "I can't go with you, but you can leave. Come on mama, please be free." I let go of her hand, but as she fell, I could still see a reflection in her eyes. As she fell back into the darkness, I realized, I was myself, but myself was her in me.

Nightmares are dreams that show you the ugly truth of what you're hiding deep inside. Whether it is fears, anxieties, or in my case resentment. I could not remember my mother's face, since she departed my life at such an early age. But this recurring nightmare made me see her more clearly. There was so much resentment I had buried deep inside my soul. It manifests as the tough girl I could only pretend to be. We are doomed to repeat history if we do not learn from it and do things to change it. The same goes with a curse.

~

'Breathe in. Breathe out. Brea-...screw it, they're gonna get rocked today!'

That is what crossed my mind several times as I fought through my childhood. I was a war dog under the illusion that everyone and everything was against me. I wore this rage like a mink coat in the winter, and a crop top in the summer. It was present for all the world to see. I was fighting people, running away from foster homes, and one day got locked up in juvenile detention. I was screaming for people to pay attention to a resentment I was not ready to deal with. All I wanted and needed was to be loved unconditionally, but unfortunately, I was a problem and a paycheck.

Even so I had to forgive. Easier said than done. How was I supposed to look someone in the face who took care of me for the sake of their car note, I mean rent, I mean a lifestyle, and say I forgive you? One day I was walking on the boardwalk in Far Rockaway, swatting away the thug seagulls and black birds who *thought* I had food. Then every memory started to play in my head like an old school Busta Rhymes video. I could see the faces I scratched, eyes I blackened, arms I bruised, and ears I screamed out in my rage, all in vibrant technicolor. I kept seeing it over and over again and my walk became a sashay of vengeance empowered by fury – fury that I felt justified to have. Then everything darkened around me and I saw my mother reaching her way out of the well to grab me once more.

I stopped dead in my tracks, shook uncontrollably and cried. I needed to forgive everyone, but first I needed to forgive myself. This concept was foreign to me, but I dare not see the well woman again. There was no prayer I could say that would dissipate the fear in my heart. So, I resorted to going with what I knew. The war dog needed to seek comfort with a man who understood God. I hopped on the train and hurried myself to my church on Merrick Boulevard and pleaded with my pastor for counsel.

He walked me to his office. It reminded me of a refurbished library. It had mahogany bookshelves filled with books. Across from the bookshelves were two padded cherrywood chairs on a beige carpet. I settled myself in a chair. He patiently sat across from me listening to my joys about finding family, and my anxiety about the curse to fail within my bloodline. Pastor sat with his hands folded as if he were going to give me some bad news and said,

"Felicia, I want to congratulate you on starting your healing process. It is not going to be easy. You will need to embrace the truth of your past, be open to the wisdom gained from your experiences, have faith that God is working all of this for your good, and conjure the courage to forgive. As you continue to be enlightened about who you are as a woman you must learn to trust her as you will trust others. Use discernment as you open yourself to new possibilities and know that as you heal it is well within your soul."

I nodded, but was confused and said, "So...what do I do?"

Pastor chuckled and said, "Well you can start by asking for forgiveness from those you may have hurt while you were hurting. Then maybe see who else you need to forgive so that you can be healed. God is on your side and knows that you will endure."

I took a deep breath and nodded in agreement and walked out of the church. A black cat was sitting at the bottom of the church steps and stared at me as I walked down. As I continued down the street the cat followed me. I kept saying I didn't have food for it, but the cat kept following me as I walked along the block. When I turned to cut through the alley the cat sat and watched me walk away. It looked sad to see me go. It was kind of beautiful as the sun shone on its fur through the car window parked behind it.

"I'll be alright. Thanks for walking with me." I waved and said.

I turned the corner and started to think more about what Pastor said. Admitting you are wrong is unheard of in the Black household. Apologies come in the form of extra food on a plate, an offer of a favor, or staring at each other and hoping someone can telepathically understand your remorse until you just start talking. Well, I had no food or favors to offer and certainly was not a mutant with telepathic powers. So, I did the hard walk in my *"timbs"* and my sneakers and marched to the homes I was transitioning through and hoped that they would listen.

I knocked on a door in Brooklyn and said, "I was a little girl hurting and trying to find my way in life."

I knocked on a door in Manhattan and said, " I didn't know how to love and it made me bitter."

I knocked on a door in Queens and said, "I was angry and afraid to trust people."

They all seemed to understand and peacefully closed their doors and sent me on my way.

Then I knocked on a door in Wyandanch and said, "Just know that I am ok, and I made it. I am no longer angry about you sending me away. I understand that you did what you felt was best for me."

And my foster mother, Marian said, " I never thought I would see you again." Then she gave me a grandmother hug that let me know that she was happy I was alive, well, and reassured me that if I was not ok I surely would be.

The reality of it all was that Marian loved me. She treated me exactly how she treated her own children. As we continued to talk and reminisce about old times I wrapped my arms around her and said,

"Ma, I forgive you and I hope you forgive me for mistaking you as my enemy when all you wanted to do was love me and give me what I was missing. A loving home that re-assured me that the love and support was always going to be there."

From that day forward, no one could tell me that we weren't family, or at least connected. I continued my counseling sessions with Pastor who continued t guide me through my forgiveness process. God was showing me it was about me being able to move on in the future and embrace my purpose here on earth. As I began forgiving those foster parents and asking for my own forgiveness, I started to feel light on my feet but also in my heart.

Then there was one more person to forgive. My blood source.

~

I walked back to the valley as myself and this time it was not a dream, nor a nightmare. The brisk graveyard air scampered across my face as my feet did the same on the uneven yellowing grass that caught the shadows of passing clouds. As I inched closer to the grave, the simple concrete slab transformed into the well from which the creature would grab me. I shook off the vision and stood atop my mother's hallowed ground. Then the fear of losing what little I had to the demons of her past took over.

I city marched, like I was trying to catch a train, away from her grave. Suddenly, the memory of my foster mother who wrapped her arms around me and said, "*I never thought I'd see you again*," made me pause. What if the whole time my mother was fighting to get out of the well, she was trying to see me again. Perhaps so we could talk, maybe a warning, or to say I'm sorry. But instead of listening, I painted her as the monster because in my most vivid memory of her, that is what she was. I took a deep breath and sauntered to her grave.

There atop that block of stone she sat barefoot in her frayed jeans, a red and black-striped shirt, and the twinkle of early evening light reflecting on her almond skin and longing eyes. She had waited for this day for a long time and now was time for me to tell her the truth.

"Ma. Beverly. I want to let you know that I'm alright. I remember you mostly as the monster that I hid from in the closet, somehow also the only one I could trust. There were times I'd raise my arms to your disquieted face hoping my love would cure the pain from the one you loved, Mr. Fix...or also my father. Yet when you could have answered in love your response was to instantly vanish back into your darkness."

Beverly stood up and shook with a tear streaming down her face, disheartened that I only remembered her as a monster. I halted her emotions and continued,

"Do you remember the day my life ended with you? You were in yet another drug infused rage along with my father. He threw a beer bottle across the room and hit my forehead. Before they took me away, you became my mother. Mr. Fix had no grasp on your maternal instinct to cradle me, hum a song, and let me know that I was going to be alright."

Beverly coyly smirked and sat back down wrapping her arms around herself as if to hold a baby. Tears welled up in her eyes and reflected the daylight as the night slowly started to gently pull it away. I lowered my eyes, sighed and my anger built up with every word I spoke,

"I was four. I was four when people in tattered skirts and worn shirts took me away from you and when Mr. Fix took you away from me. You don't know what grief is when you're so young. I didn't know how to miss you and processing that all these years smacked me in the face with anger, resentment, bewilderment, apathy and rage! My soul knew that you, my mother was gone, but my mind could not process the thought of being in this world alone for the decades!-"

Beverly quivered at my rage then swiftly stood to her feet and inched closer to me and stared into my eyes. Her lips did not move, but her eyes were tear-filled and for the first time I could hear her soothing song-like voice,

"I remember that you were the best part of me and there was nothing I could do but give you a chance. I had to let you go. God was done with me in His plans because I threw away all my chances. It could have been better for you and it could have been worse. Give yourself a chance to be the best part of God's plan."

As the sun set behind her she was being pulled away by the last strings of light coming through the trees. She stumbled as she fought to stand on the grave to hear what I had to say. My lips quivered and my cheeks were overrun with tears knowing that my mother loved me after all, under all the drugs and pain. I smiled through my tears and said,

"I love you Beverly. I forgive you."

As the last twinkle of light was losing its battle to hang on to the branch of a sole tree, it twinkled on my mother's joyful smile as she faded away with the light.

Be well.

JASMINE, CHIKE, & IFE

GOD, I WAS not, but a full-on goddess I was being! I was too blessed to be stressed, job having, suburb living, and money moves making. Smiling brighter than Times Square with a sway that moved haters out my way like air. You could see me, the art on the wall, a woman from whom grace did not fall. You could feel my vibe from New Haven to Jersey City. Ready to conquer the world and no matter what I kept smiling. I was lost to tell you the truth. No one could see that I was bruised from the shattered dreams of what life could be. Hot dammit, I was broke and adulting!

I had moved out of Josephine's house and had gotten my first job with benefits as an administrator for a youth detention center, and my first apartment in Queens out in Rosedale where the islanders live the American dream. I figured for a chick fresh off of the foster care assembly line I was doing really well. But guess what BS they did not put in my *how-to-adult* brochure? How to manage money! If someone put a checklist of adulting-correctly in front of me I could only check the box that said ***by pure dumb luck I am still alive***. Every day when I sashayed my way to work, I'd hear the echo of my counselors *What are your intentions with your life?* To that very day the answer remained the same, *how the hell should I know? I'm alive and I'm adulting.*

∼

Every morning, I'd scarf whatever food that was in my hands

reach into my mouth on my way out the door. Sometimes it was instant oatmeal that I'd spill on my shirt. If I got up in time, it was homemade bacon egg and cheese. On my bill weeks, it was a banana that I pretended was a four-course meal. Nevertheless, I'd swing my coat on like Shaft then scuttle my way out of Rosedale on the E train and sit among the other adults trying to get it right. I'd put on headphones at Jamaica station and drown out the world until 7th Ave. Then snatch them out while running to catch the D train to 145th, so I'd make it up the hill in Harlem in time to greet the trauma of foster youth that became my soundtrack for the day.

One morning, the working woman-scuttle shuffle felt off. I felt like something was creeping behind me over my shoulders. When I hopped on the train, I dangled my arm from that questionably clean rail above me, took a breath and said here we go. My paranoia would not rest. I used my arm as a peek-a-boo shield to look around at every suspect, I mean person, on the train waiting to fight. When we got to each stop, I'd look at the reflection in the window to peek at the people behind me. I saw a Dominican chick with pink headphones too happy before coffee rocking out behind me and a White girl leaning by the door in a green hooded jacket eerily giving the girl in the headphones a side eye and looking back at her phone. All of this seemed normal to me, yet I still felt like something was coming.

The final stretch of my 15-minute ride from 7th Ave to 145th felt like an hour being packed in with every other anxious New Yorker afraid they'll miss their coffee before they hit the desk. There were no escape routes, and I was counting down the stops hoping I would miss whatever was about to pop off. Then when we arrived at 125th street there was a rustle on the microphone followed by a groan throughout the train and a unified chant with the conductor of

"There is a delay."

The conductor continued on, "We have police activity ahead of us and will be moving once the matter is resolved."

My anxiety started confirming my worst fears. *This is it. This is the day I die. What do they mean police activity? Can they chase him to the next station so we can move?*

Suddenly a man shouted, "Yo! Can they just scrape his ass off of the tracks? We need to get to work!"

I didn't know whether to be horrified at his assumption of suicide and complete disregard of it or that whatever was happening was about to come on to this train. I saw the cops take a guy off the train and people grumbled until we got moving again. I finally got to 145th street and pushed my way through the crowd. As I just cleared the doors, I felt someone grab my arm and say, *"Hey!"* I ripped away from their grasp and turned to see the white girl in the green hood.

"The hell is wrong with you?! What?!" I shouted

Her hood covered her eyes and all I could see was her lips quivering as she tried to work up the courage to speak. She finally said, "I'm sorry it took so long."

"What?" I replied with a face warped in confusion.

"I'm sorry it took so long for us to arrive," she said with a smirk.

I raised an eyebrow and said, "Ok! Well, we're here now... thanks, I think."

I turned around and hustled up the stairs then on to my march up to the hill to the New York Juvenile Detention Center. Or as I called it in my mind, Sugar Hill House for Wayward Kids.

Sugar Hill House was a castle built for the petty thieves trying to survive, the runaways who thought they'd thrive, and the school skippers that found better things to do with their time. The walls were painted with their grievances and their traumas seeped through floors. You'd never know that there was so much pain inside of the beautiful brownstone building; I could relate.

The red clay castle housed youth that were aged 12-16 and was nestled next to a charter school that looked like a marble church and a church that looked like a remix of the Alamo. I loved the vibe of the detention center. The first floor had a kitchen and multi-purpose room that was decorated with art created by the students. This gave them such a connection to their souls. The house had space for many youths on two floors with the management office in the basement.

Whenever I'd walk in the house, I was ready to help those kids heal from things that I had not healed from myself yet. I figured if I could save them by being a counselor or trainer, then I could save a piece of myself every day. By being in that house, I had a chance of redeeming my own traumas vicariously through them. I was abandoned just like them. I suffered from depression just like them. I battled stigmas just like them. I was them. So, every day that I touched those grieving walls and walked the sorrowful wood panels the house would whisper, *welcome home*. Today it had a new message as I walked into the common room and one of the young men Eric, was posted up by the affirmations mirror on the wall rapping to a group of his friends,

'Life is a ride, don't get mesmerized by the chains, false prophets, and sweet lies that be all up between your thighs, make you cry 'bout somebody worthless, that ain't divine.'

"Boy!" I interjected "Nice flow, but Eric what you know about life is a ride talking about somebody all up between your thighs?! You better not be all up in somebody thighs." I scolded trying to hold back a smile.

"I'm just speaking my mind, Ms. Wilson. I woke up today feeling spiritual! Wanted to drop some knowledge on these youngins," Eric said charmingly as he flicked his chain.

My eyebrow rose looking at his chain and I said, "Eric you're not supposed to have jewelry. Where did you get that?"

"This lady came by, like maybe 15 minutes ago, and dropped this off. She said it was a gift for me. I don't have to give it up, do I Ms. Wilson?" Eric asked with pleading eyes.

I put my hand out to demand it. He sighed and handed it over. "You know you can't have that; give it here. You can have it back when you leave." I huffed to center myself and get ready for the day, "Ok, line up for the head count and then we'll do our *real* rap session."

I continued my day per usual; handing out medication, processing paperwork for new delinquents, going over educational enhancements for the youth who were attending school. I felt like I was making a real difference and hoped that none of these kids would end up feeling like they had to turn back to crime or drugs to escape their pasts. I was called into the manager's office and with humble gratitude for my services they informed me that they had some budget cuts and I made the list of the people to be downgraded from an administrator to a counselor.

After they told me that my position was being downgraded again to a counselor then my paranoia was lifted. This is what was coming. It was only an unexpected shift; not a big deal. Then my anxiety flared up with thoughts like, "If I had done a better job would they have kept me in the position and fought for my salary? Maybe I'm not good enough and never will be. Have I done nothing to change these kids' lives?"

While I sat in the multipurpose room racking my brain with all of the possibilities one of the former youths, Anjolie, burst into the house and she yelled,

"Ms. Wilson! Ms. Wilson!"

Anjolie walked through the house and found me in the multipurpose room. She stood there gleaming with pride with her high school diploma in hand. I looked at what she had and before I could say a word she leapt into my arms and hugged me. She thanked me for my counsel and guidance through her time in the house and was looking to dream big. I encouraged her to do so and never accept no for an answer. It didn't matter what my position was, I was making a difference. But with this budget cut I was going to need another job.

~

The person who sees through your best and worst self and always sees the beauty in your soul, is your best friend in the world. That is what I had in Jasmine. She would see me celebrating or losing it and smile to let me know it would be alright. I called her Sis.

Sis and I met at a mutual friend's house in Jamaica, Queens during the summer of 2002. It was one of the first summer house parties I had gone to, when I was partially free from foster care. She strutted in the house in a skirt, sneakers, and cute top, hugging everyone hello. She ran over to me with the giddiest "let's be friends" smile. I didn't trust her at first, but we started talking about college, cute guys at the party, and she eventually dragged me outside to dance to Nelly's, *Hot In Here*, and forced me to embrace the vibe of a hot day in the city. Of course, my shyness took over and I went to go sit on the front steps. Sis came to find me outside and asked me to walk with her to bodega down the street.

While we were walking down the street these drunk guys were slow riding down the street yelling out their cars for us to come over. We kept walking and they kept following us. I was ready to fight, but Jasmine told me to keep walking until we got to the bodega. We ducked inside the bodega and saw a black manager cat chilling up on top of a radio while Linkin Park played. He looked like he was nodding to the song. Jasmine and I laughed and walked to get a bottle of juice.

When we opened the refrigerator door one of the guys from the car ran up into the store yelling *'Eh...eh! You hear me talking to you! I said come here!'* Part of me wanted to fight but the other said to hide because he was twice my size. He charged towards us, despite the bodega owner yelling at the unruly guy to leave. Sis chucked a big glass bottle of Mystic Blue at his head and as he fell back the manager cat jumped on his face and started scratching him up. We ran and jumped over the guy screaming in anguish and out the door and the bodega owner was cussing us out the whole time. We ran back towards the party and by the time we got there we could not stop laughing. We've been making trouble ever since wherever we went, but we always had each other's back.

One night I slept over at her house and had the nightmare about my mother and kept screaming. She woke me up and without judgement or question, rocked me in her arms and told me,

"As long as I'm around nothing will hurt you. And if it does it'll have to put up a helluva fight to get through me and to get through you. You're much stronger than your mother. She's not going to get you. I promise."

It felt great to have someone say that to me after years of people not caring if I screamed, cried, or died. There was nothing I couldn't tell her and worry about judgement and today was no different. I called her up when I got home from my long day of paranoia that turned out to just being downsized. She cackled,

"Girl, why are you walking around like somebody got a hit out on you?! They're just cheap."

"I woke up today and felt this gloom over me," I replied chuckling. "Like someone was watching me. I kept reaching for my mace and shit."

"Well, I guess you live to see another day!" Sis laughed, "Hey I have my niece on Saturday. If you're not dead, you want to go shopping?"

We cackled and I replied, "Sure."

That Saturday she rolled her two-year-old niece up to the Beach Ave house in her bulky stroller that her niece *just had* to have. I shook my head telling Sis that there was no way we were going to make it on the Q85 bus with that sports car of a stroller. In her usual enthusiasm she said,

"We'll be fine! People will move, we'll be *aight*."

I shook my head, and we took off down the street playing airplane with the stroller zooming down the street so her niece would be entertained. We made it over to Jamaica Ave and snatched up some sneakers, shirts, and some food that we couldn't finish. All of it ended up in the bottom of the stroller. The stroller was so puffy at the bottom it dragged as we pushed it. I was so annoyed because I knew it was not going to fit on the bus.

We got on the bus and she held her niece and sat in front of the bus. I was seated right across from her on the opposite side holding the overstuffed stroller. The stroller was one of the objects that was bulky and had two snaps on the side where you had to pull it up and it folded in half. The bus begins moving and the stroller started rolling back and forth. I immediately became agitated and start arguing with Jasmine about why we should have taken the cheaper fold-up stroller, but she argued back that we would have had to carry all the bags.

When we approached our stop to get off an older lady was trying to exit the bus as well and stumbled over the stroller! I had to catch her then get the puffy stroller off the bus and help the old lady walk. I was cussing Sis out the whole time we exited the bus for not listening to me about this huge stroller to the point that it became inaudible.

"Youcouldakilltheoldass-y-youshouldalistentome! Canteven-putthedamnbabyinthecar-stroller! YaknowwhatImean!" I yelled then grabbed a pair of the shoes from the stroller and threw them down the street and marched off.

Jasmine's niece started to giggle, and it worked up to an infectious laughter. I turned around and Sis erupted in a contagious laughter and I joined in. I grabbed the shoes and walked back to them and Jasmine laughed,

"Girl! You really need to work on your anger. It is well. The lady didn't fall, and we didn't have to carry all these bags."

After we walked to drop off her niece, we wandered around Queens carrying the ten bags we had stuffed in her stroller. She loved New York in the fall so much, although I hated it. It was wet, all the leaves were dying, and it smelled like death and smog. Next to her though, even all this death that surrounded us had some spark of life. She adored it so much that if the wind lifted a small pile of leaves, she'd dance in it and force me to dance too. Moments like that made us forget how much we may have been struggling.

We were almost to her building. An Asian woman in a blue hoodie started marching towards us. Jasmine looked like she recognized her. As the woman got closer, she and Sis exchanged an acknowledging look. I immediately asked,

"Who is that?! Why is she staring you down? We got a problem. I'll drop these bags!"

Jasmine laughed and pulled me along towards her building, "It's fine; just someone I know from around my way."

We got right outside her building and she looked like she was going to cry. Sis took a breath and said,

"I gotta go."

I was confused, "Huh? Inside? Yeah, I know it's getting cold, let's go."

"I'm not going to make it if I stay in this city, "Sis teared up and continued, "There is this position in Job Corps upstate an-an-and…"

I exploded, "You leaving?! You're leaving me Jasmine! For real?! Come on; this is New York City. You can make yourself into anything here. You've done so much; you can…"

Sis grabbed and hugged me, "Licia… I have to go. You and I are two different kinds of strong. You can take this city because you're built for it, and I'm built for something else."

She let me go and I sobbed, "But we were supposed to do this together. Our kids are supposed to be best friends! Remember we'd live around the corner from each other, so they always had homes to go to. We had plans! You can't do this!"

"Felicia! I want the absolute best for you and even though you won't say it now you want that for me too." Sis said.

We dropped our bags, embraced tightly and sobbed. The tears that ran down our cheeks. I could tell she was waiting for me to say something that approved her leaving to start her life. Sis couldn't leave. She was the only one that let me know that it was ok to be me for better or worse. I mustered up the strength to be supportive and said,

"So how did you find the job?"

Sis chuckled, "Walked into a recruiting office and applied"

"That's it?" I replied

Sis got flustered and said, "Fine I confess! I rode the recruiter's lap like a hungry stripper until he said, "Ok, ok; you're hired!"

We both cackled, put our arms around each other's shoulders, and continued walking down the street.

Two weeks went by and my job decided to let me go for budget cut reasons. After a stint of job searching, I begrudgingly helped Sis get to Penn Station. The whole time I was replaying all of our adventures through my head. It was like watching a recap of our favorite shows all blended into one. I know she was talking to me, but I was like a zombie. Here I was alone in the world, no job, no plans, and my friend was abandoning me for greener pastures. It wasn't until we got to the station and I took her as far as I could that I finally heard her say,

"Hey, Lecia. You're extraordinary. Don't forget that."

I nodded, "Jasmine…" I took a deep sigh to hide my rising sadness and continued, "I don't know what you're going to do. I don't know what I'm going to do. But whatever it is, we're going to kick ass."

We nodded, hugged, had one last look at the women we were leaving behind and drifted away from each other. I shuffled away and made my way out to 6th Ave. By the time I made it outside, everything looked black and white. I couldn't hear the angry drivers, I barely saw the people walking around me, and couldn't feel the rumble of the trains underneath my feet. I started to hyperventilate, and the sadness took over my body. I collapsed into my hands and sobbed.

This is what was waiting around the corner for me, the end of my safe place.

Dammit.

~

I wish women knew from an early age how to be their own best friend. I had been in survival mode for so long that I didn't know how to confide in myself. But now it was time as, sis would say, *'Get your soul 'n shit straight'.*

For the next few weeks, I searched for part-time jobs to supplement my income from the detention center. I had to dumb down my resume a little bit so it wouldn't show my college degree and prove that I needed a job in the worst way. I would talk to Jas when she had time and after every call she would say 'Get your soul n shit straight'. One day I took her advice and walked into a Rite Aid and looked through all the notebooks wondering which one would be perfect to write down my life plan. Such a trivial thing, it's just paper; but if my life was going to be extraordinary, I needed a notebook to match. Finally, I found a small purple notebook and hurried home to start writing.

Well, when I got there I laid down on my bed and stared up at the ceiling running every scenario through my head about how great I could be. *Maybe I'll be a business owner. Perhaps a millionaire. Or I can marry rich.* Then suddenly all of these negative images of my past and Beverly flooded my mind. I sat up on my bed, screamed, and broke down into tears. Once I calmed down, I began to write:

I need to be spiritually stable - *Well, go to church.*

I need to be mentally stable - *I need a therapist.*

I need money to pay for a therapist - *Need a better job.*

If I want a better job and to make an impact I need to go back to school.

I paused my writing to envision myself in the future. I saw a woman dressed in a suit running programs that will help foster care youth shift gears into adulthood while becoming their own leaders in different fields of their personal and professional lives. Neither one of my parents completed high school let alone got a college degree. I went on to further my education and break down the stigma attached to the family I knew.

I realized how much I had to offer to change my circumstances. I knew that I needed to prevail through hard and consistent work. I needed to let go of the life I was born into for me to live my best life now. I had to be the one willing to create the path of where I wanted to go. Unfortunately, I still didn't know how I was going to get there. I did know that I needed to change my mindset and how I felt others perceived me. I knew I had to do what I had never done or was willing to do before. I had to take a leap of faith.

My thoughts made me pace around the room in a perpetual maddening state of overthinking. If my feet were cement, I would have cracked a hole in my neighbor's ceiling. Eventually I passed out on the couch. Then suddenly I woke up and was on the side of a mountain road along the coast overlooking the sea. The highway lined the mountain as you would see in a James Bond movie. It was neither night nor day, just a calming sky through which the dark blue ocean peeked through. I kicked the dusty gravel around my feet and continuously paced, just trying to figure out how the hell I got on the side of a mountain at the butt crack of dawn.

"Yo, am I upstate?" I said aloud.

Suddenly a black couple hugged the curve of the windy road in a light blue Cadillac as they zipped their way towards me. The man whipped the car in front of me with the back of the car nearly missing my thighs as he pulled up. The license plate read Imani. The man wore a white shirt that reflected the vibrancy of his mahogany pearl skin and blue jeans. As he lowered his sunglasses, he flashed a smile and revealed his hazel eyes. The woman leaned back and flung her Senegalese twists over the headrest. Her smooth mocha skin, plump red lips, and gleaming smile were accentuated with her entire jogger outfit. The outfit reminded me of the Puerto Rican girls who throw on some pants and a tank top to run out, but always looked cute.

She opened the car door and insisted I get in. Before I could answer, the red lady snatched me into the car and shoved me into the backseat. As the pearl man continued to drive up the windy roads on the mountainside, the red lady turned around and put her knees in the seat to face me. The wind played with her twists and tossed them around her head as she pulled a blunt from her pocket. She placed it between her elegantly delicate finger and lit it with a torch flame lighter. She rested the bright white blunt between her lips and took the first draw as if to give the blunt a kiss. Lady red smiled at me as smoke escaped her plump lips and calmly said,

"You want a hit?"

"No" I sternly said, "Who the hell are you? I don't know what that is. I'm not smoking on that shit!"

She coyly smiled at me as she took another hit and said, "I'm Ife." She held up the blunt and continued, "And this, I call this faith."

The car continued its upward climb through the air. As we inched our way up the highway , Ife continued to smoke and smile at me. Chike turned on the radio and *Heaven Is in The Backseat of My Cadillac* started playing. I remember hearing this at one of my foster homes. They played it over and over again when they were trying to hide that they were drunk.

Ife turned back around and began dancing in the front seat raising the blunt in the air as Chike did a funky nod. I became increasingly uneasy and started looking for ways to safely jump out of the car. Then Ife took a big drag of the blunt, crawled onto Chike's lap and kissed him as if they were about to make love. They shared the smoke between their lips and most of it blew back on me. I waved the smoke away as Ife laughed and said,

"You remember this one baby. We had some times in this Cadillac huh?!"

She hopped off his lap and scooted on her knees back to her seat. She offered me the blunt again with a big smile on her face. I shook my head. Ife laughed and tossed the blunt to me, spun around facing forward then launched herself backward. The pearl man caught her by her ankle with his right hand and kept driving the convertible with the other. Ife smiled as she waved her arms with the sway of her body.

"Are you crazy! I'm not dying up here over your stupid ass!" I screamed the entire time as she gleefully dangled on the back of the car.

The pearl man stopped the car on a straightaway at the top of the mountain. Ife swung her body towards me and reached for my arms to pull her in. She gave me a hug, smiled, and said,

"Thanks for holding on to faith and picking me up."

"You're welcome...I think." I got flustered and shouted at the driver "And who the hell are you?!"

The pearl man chuckled and said in a Brooklyn accent, "I'm Chike. Are you ready Felicia?"

"Ready for what?" I snapped aggressively.

"It's time for you to embrace it, sweetheart," Chike continued.

"You need to take a hit baby," Ife said as she tried to push my hand to take a hit of the blunt. She continued, "Chike is taking us on a ride. But I promise I will be with you all the way. Don't be scared."

"Where the hell are we going?"

Ife hopped into the front seat as Chike revved the engine. I belligerently asked again, *"where are we going?!"* Chike and Ife said in unison,

"On your journey."

He floored the gas pedal and we sped up the straightaway and off the edge of the cliff! As the car glided through the air I thought, *"this is it, this is it, this is how I die. No one knows I'm here; no one can bury me. Jas is gonna be pissed!"* Then Chike spoke,

"Have faith in the power of your journey."

Ife sat up on her knees and turned to face me as the convertible careened down towards an open field. With the wind whipping her twists around, she grabbed my face and smiled as she whispered,

"This is love."

...then we crashed onto the open field.

HOLDING WATER // FELICIA R. WILSON

SUNFLOWER CHILD

When you come to know yourself, you become your own source of power. But if you will not know yourself, you will dwell in an eternity of poverty; it is you who is that impoverished place.

~

My eyes shot open and I leapt off my couch. I stumbled over my shoes and fell to the ground. I anxiously felt for the wholeness of my limbs and body. I panted and tried to slow my breathing down by reminding myself, *"It was just a dream; it was just a dream."* I laughed in relief. It built up to pure hysterics when I realized that I must've been getting a contact high from my self-proclaimed Rasta neighbors that smoked the half-oregano, half-bud mix. It was just a dream, just a dream.

do-do-do-dee-do!

My phone blared that annoying generic ringtone they have on prepaid phones that made me jump out of my skin. A department store in Manhattan finally called me back for an interview for a job I desperately needed. When I walked into the department store, I was surrounded by luxuries I had never seen before; nor could I afford any of it. I felt trapped in yet another fishbowl of expectations and knew I'd never be good enough. This was not my calling; nevertheless, it was a job to pay some bills.

While I shuffled through the motions of taking a one-hour commute to work for a job that barely kept me fed, I took an assessment of my life and kept making moves. Some of my family had finally been identified. I had applied to one of the top schools in the country for a Criminal Justice degree, and to my surprise I got in and was set to start in the spring! It was important for me to reach beyond my understanding of how children operated in the justice system. I could not stand by and watch someone destroy themselves. Maybe my calling was advocacy, maybe it was to be a lawyer, either way I was going to use my voice for change.

I was still trying to get right with God; I was still forgiving my mother. With all of my different shifts, forgiving my mother was the greatest thing I could do for my own healing. Unfortunately, I would never get to know her. As I continued to find more of my family, I started to feel more like myself. At the same time, I still felt lost and didn't know exactly where I came from. Although C. Levinia Moore kept contacting me, I felt like she was baiting me with tidbits of information about my family and was just trying to get to know me before she told me more. Nevertheless, I was in hustle mode.

Christmas season had finally arrived and that is when the store transformed from a luxury department store into Santa's mistress' toy store. Anything that had a lot of bling, tech, or was top of the line fashion was ready and available for the residents of the upper east side. We had to greet each customer with a smile, knowing that while they were going home with a diamond encrusted bangle bracelet, we were likely going home to buy an online knockoff that turns your skin green.

It just wasn't fair! I had done well in school, I suffered 63 foster homes, I contributed back to my community, and here I was smiling in the faces of people who didn't give a damn about me but demanded I smile for their comfort.

One day I was working the jewelry counter and I saw one of the popular animal bangles that all the women were buying. I kept staring at a gold diamond encrusted bangle that had the head of a jaguar on it and the body wrapped around the wrist. It was stunning. It was a statement. It was mine. As we began to lock up and shut down the store my manager asked me to remove the different pieces and lock them in the safe. I removed the rings, earrings, and finally the bracelets. I walked the bracelets back to the safe with my manager over my shoulder taking inventory of the other items. Another sales associate went into a frenzy when she saw a roach scamper across the floor in front of her. My manager rolled her eyes and turned to address her, ignoring me. As I slid the last of the bracelets into the safe, I grabbed the jaguar bracelet, stuffed it in my bra and closed the safe.

I was so giddy on my way home, playfully hiding my face from people who I thought would know that I stole something. When I got to my building, I ran upstairs snatched off my coat and slipped the bracelet on my left wrist and didn't take it off for three days. I cooked with it on. I showered with it on. I called random people just so I could hold my phone with my left hand and see my treasure. I may not have everything I wanted yet, but I at least had this.

The next few days at work were a breeze. I was smiling effortlessly and flirting with the customers to make them buy more of anything they wanted. The customers loved me and called me a troublemaker because I made them spend twice as much as they had intended. That Friday I went to the back office to get my check from my manager and she asked me to sit down. She turned on a small television that showed a video of me pocketing the bracelet. She turned it off, peered over her glasses and said,

"I was counting the days until you did something like this. You are going to end up right where I thought you would...in prison. Your kind are so typical. Your parents didn't want you nor did anyone else, and then you do things to not be ever wanted anywhere else. The police are outside the door. Hand over the bracelet; I know you have it."

She extended her hand demanding the bracelet and all I could do was cry; and then I took off running. There was nowhere I could run, but I went for it anyway. The police grabbed my arms and escorted me to the police car in the view of lingering customers who had come to adore me. They gasped and whispered as I passed them by and looked away if I tried to look at them.

I was transported to jail and sat in the cell with my face down in my lap. I didn't know what to expect. Then all of a sudden, I was booked and stripped down of my personal belongings, and handed bedding to carry to the juvenile unit. Because I was just released from the foster system a few months prior I still had some level of a barrier as a ward of the state. Usually, that was ignored but God was on my side.

Once I got to the housing unit, I walked over to my area and sat on the bed. The minute the door locked; I knew this had now become my reality. I started crying so hard that I could not catch my breath. I felt like my world had just caved in on me. I just knew that I was alone. I had no one I could call on. The voice of one of my foster mothers from Queens, Kima, kept ringing in my head:

"If you ever get locked up you better not call me. You have no reason to be out here acting a fool and getting yourself into any kind of trouble"

She worked for the New York City department of juvenile justice. While listening to her voice, I knew that I had not better dare to pick up the phone and attempt to call her. Well, who else was I going to call?

One thing I always knew was that Kima was that ride or die foster mother for her teenagers that were placed in her home. She was outspoken and didn't take any mess from anyone, least of all her foster children. When I called her and got no answer, I knew that she was getting tired of me and the nonsense I was getting myself into. Even though I had apologized before, she did tell me to never call her from prison. From that very moment I gave up on myself.

For the next thirteen days I witnessed bagels being heated up in the dryer to living with an unrelenting funk that smelled like a takeout place in the hood with a D rating. There were some girls that were battling bi-polar disorder, depression, and schizophrenia. The schizophrenic would scream at night before lockdown, because apparently that personality needed a burst of chaos to function properly the next day. She was never given the proper medication and the guards just let her rave to everyone's agonizing annoyance. They had us two to a small room with a toilet barely six feet away.

One night I stared at the bottom of my "roommate'" bunk and started replaying the last few days in my mind. The Wire did not prepare me for what I was enduring. There was no murder or plots...to my knowledge. But I was definitely feeling like an animal in a cage. Why was it worth it to steal? What possessed me to do things like this? I continued to berate myself for all the stupid decisions I made. Then, like clockwork the screaming started at the top of her lungs. It was the only other constant I counted on and her shrieks serenaded me to sleep.

I woke up laying in an open field that was decorated in twilight with stars peeking through the velvet sky. I jumped up and frantically spun around to check out my surroundings and saw barren trees and a void of nothingness. I tried to calm myself by closing my eyes and doing the breathing exercises our counselor tried to teach us. "I'm dreaming. I'm dreaming. This isn't real. I'm having an anxiety attack." I kept telling myself this as I slowly turned around and carefully opened my eyes. I opened up my right eye and the barren space was filled with redwood trees. I heard laughter, joyful screeching and snapped my head to my left and opened my other eye to see a carnival.

As I kept turning around, I saw the blue convertible in which I had been kidnapped. *"I'm high. I have to be. Someone put something in my food and now I'm having high dreams."* I thought to myself. All of a sudden, a melodic bird-like whistle caught my attention. I spun around and saw the same woman who kidnapped me sitting on a tree stump. As I slowly walked towards her, I examined her ornate outfit that somehow blended an old southern look with Harlem renaissance. She was dressed in a long blue, yellow, and red Kente print poodle skirt that looked like peacock feathers with a frilly black button up top. Her full-bodied, shoulder length hair was curled and held up on the side by a butterfly fascinator that allowed the rest of her it to drape on her top. I finally arrived in front of her.

"Well! Look who finally arrived. How you doing, baby?" Ife said with a smile.

"Yup! I'm high." I proclaimed

"Naw, baby you sleep. You ready to go?" Ife casually said with a friendly southern-like charm.

"I don't know where I am, I don't know who you are, or what fumes I'm inhaling right now that's making me hallucinate." I explained frantically.

Ife grabbed my hand and playfully swung it as she said, "Lawd, *honey* you are so anxious. You're safe here, sugalump. I'm your auntie. And this, this is Tribeland." She stretched out her arms like a car show girl, gleaming as she continued, "This whole place is our little corner of the spiritual realm where we can come together, speak soul to soul, watch our descendants, and advocate for people like yourself."

"Ok, I'm trippin'. I'm dreaming. I'm seeing it but I know I'm dreaming; this can't be real." I said.

"Dreams ain't nothing but an open space for your mind, heart, and soul to congregate together. It's a gateway to the spiritual realm they don't teach you much about in the church house. I don't know why you young ones can't believe in nothing. You always need some kinda proof. Isn't your faith your proof?" Ife chuckled as she got up and elegantly embraced me.

I argued, "Faith is believing in something you know is real! This is-"

"This is real ain't it?" Ife smiled and chortled.

She linked up to my arm and we casually walked towards the carnival.

"Aw, you not ready for all that yet. Anyway, did you have fun with your cousin? She's a wild one." Ife said

"Who is my cousin?" I asked.

"The girl you drove up the mountainside with and did the Evil Knievel trick with in a convertible. That's your cousin, Illeri; she's a wild one." Ife explained.

I pushed away and bucked towards her shouting, "No, that was you! You just said you are my auntie! So, which is it? Are you my auntie or my cousin?

Ife coyly rolled her eyes and put her hands on her hips as she sassily explained, "Baby, I'm your auntie, your cousin, your mama, your mee maw, great grand, all of 'em. I am every woman that is connected to your bloodline. We may all look like this, but we all have different spirits all huddled together in this one body. We are Ife. It was your cousin's crazy idea to drive you up the mountain. It was my idea to bring you to Tribeland."

"Wait..." I paused, then quivered as I said, "You're my mom too...Bev...Beverly?"

Ife took a deep solemn breath and said, "Bev isn't strong enough to talk yet. But she here. She'll get stronger, I promise." She perked up and continued, "Come on; we 're gonna go see folk. They know you coming."

Ife linked up with me again and we casually walked through the fair grounds. We saw people of every shade delighted to be among one another. We passed by a merry-go-round with real horses racing around it with people riding them and yelling their own version of yeehaw. We made our way through picnic tables where everyone was either bursting with laughter or tears. Some children scurried past us then ran into a mirror that reacted as if a rock was dropped in a pond.

"What is all this?" I asked

"It's Tribeland. I told you what we do here already, girl!" Ife laughed.

"I mean the people. The horses...the weird-ass freakshow mirror."

Ife pointed over to various groups and explained, "Ah, well. These people at the tables have relatives in them that have just crossed over that are still getting to know the place. Or they're just two different clans catching up for better or worse. The horse folk look like they're playing, but they are running around in that circle because their souls still aren't ready to deal with their pain or pain they caused. They rotate between that awful well and up here on these horses until they process. Them things hurt, but all they can do is ride around and get a glimpse of the life they can have if they just let go of the hurt."

"What about the babies?" I asked

Ife looked sad and said, "Unfortunately, those are people who crossed over long before their time and are still running back to the other side to be a part of the lives of the people they've left behind. You ever be all alone and suddenly felt like someone is rubbing up against you? That's probably one of them trying to get through." She paused and chuckled, "Mature souls pop through sometimes too and reflect their souls onto any living thing. As long as there is a mirror or anything that offers a reflection they can come on through and attach their souls to any living thing and communicate - people, house plants, kitty cats. Ha!"

"That's some creepy shit Auntie," I said.

"Hey, I don't make the rules. Come on." Ife pulled me along.

We walked towards a red and yellow big top tent with the roaring and cheers of crowds inside. As we entered, I swear I heard Bernie Mac telling jokes. I broke away from my auntie and ran towards his voice to see him. I peeked over people's shoulders only to see that it wasn't him. It was his voice, but not him. This man was slender, had a big nose, and an even bigger smile. My auntie peeked over my shoulder and chuckled,

"Oh, Bernie here today?! That man's whole tribe is funny! We come in here from time to time to tell stories about our glory days on earth or perform our songs, dance or whatever the collective soul wants to do. Sometimes it's to watch our descendants do something incredible. We discuss our family issues too; whether between our own descendants or another tribe's."

Suddenly a deranged woman with unkempt locs and disheveled clothes grabbed my arm! We tussled for thirty seconds before Ife's hand glowed a white light and she smacked the woman ten feet away from me. Ife dusted off her hands and I shouted,

"What the hell?!"

"That was the Lolonyo tribe. And the snake that grabbed you was someone in them that I haven't forgiven yet." Ife stated as we kept walking through the big top.

"Who?" I asked

"The one who sold your mother's final fix to her." Ife stated with a stern face.

I lowered my eyes, took a breath and said, "So, what is this place exactly?"

"I told you it's Tribeland. I know you are trying to figure out if this is heaven, hell, or something in between. Heaven is a vast space. This is a part of it. A lot goes on with the workings of God and it's because we are all a part of it," Ife explained as she hooked on to my arm. We continued to walk under the tent.

"What do you mean?" I asked.

Ife continued "It means, baby, that we are all a piece of God in our own way. We are all a part of different tribes, like it says in the old bible. And we all have our own place in that tribe. Ultimately, we are all of one flesh, we just look different that's all."

"If you're all a part of God, then how do you have hate for another part of God?" I asked

Ife grinned and said, "I'm still a spiritual being having a human experience, gimme a break."

"You said you're my Auntie, right?" I asked

"Yeah huh." Ife answered we shuffled through the crowd.

"Well then what's your name?" I asked

"Eva. Maiden name Malone, Married Name Thomas." She answered then continued, "My Momma had a whole farm's worth of babies." Eva laughed. "Come on here with me, suga."

We continued walking through the big top tent and I could barely keep up with what I was seeing. The entire place was set up like the Chelsea Market with different booths and rooms. I saw some people playing dice and cards in one room we passed. Another where people were having a dance battle in front of mirrors, inspiring their descendants on the other side of the mirror. We walked around the corner and there was an old-fashioned call center with numbers as high as the top of the tent and people were floating in front of the numbers punching them.

Auntie Eva explained that spirit bodies were communicating messages through coded numbers to their descendants. Across from them was a library with people speaking or singing into blank books; Ife explained that those books hold all the old and new ideas of different tribes and they are providing divine inspiration hoping their descendants *get the idea*. Then suddenly I heard cheers from other rooms and ran over to see other spiritual bodies watching ten different big screens that had a show, performance or movie on starring several of the spirits' descendants. I saw singers of all types, comics, dancers, and people making speeches .

Spirits ran past us fooling around, singing, and laughing together and I screeched and jumped. My Auntie laughed at my reaction and pulled me along. We walked up to a table covered in purple velvet with varying types of ornate jewelry that different people were touching. As they touched them the jewelry would glow, and they would talk to it and get brighter as they spoke. A Latina woman sat behind the table dressed in a mid-length purple off the shoulder sundress with an ornate multicolored necklace and long hair surrounding her high cheekbones. She was holding a long skinny fork watching the patrons intently as they approached the jewelry. Auntie Eva pulled me close and whispered into my ear,

"Now this is Mrs. Colibri. She is tasked with providing access to the divine copies of jewelry they left behind for loved ones. Spirit bodies come by and bless the different pieces so that when their descendant wears it an anointing will be on them. They picked a pretty terrible guide for such things; she's mean."

"So, if someone puts a necklace or watch from their ancestor they'll be blessed. Interesting. What's with the fork?" I asked.

Ife winced and said, "She pokes people with it if they don't need to be touching the jewelry."

Suddenly Mrs. Colibri snapped her head to the left and scurried over to a Japanese man, raised the fork two feet above her head as it glowed white and she impaled the man's hand! An electric shock from the fork made the man jump back from the table as she shouted,

"I told you to stop coming here! You're bad luck! Every time you touch that ring something bad happens to your niece. Who let you off the horse? You're still not right. Vayase!"

Eva giggled and whispered, "See."

Mrs. Colibri slowly turned around and walked back to her seat as she looked us up and down and said, "Eva...are you lying to that girl about me."

Eva readjusted herself into a ladylike stance and said, "No, ma'am I am not."

Mrs. Colibri sucked her teeth and said, "Mentirosa." They laughed and hugged each other, and she continued, "So this is your niece, huh? Nice to meet you mama. Is your auntie showing you around?"

I coyly chuckled, "Yes, ma'am she is. I'm not sure I'm supposed to be seeing all this."

Mrs. Colibri was bewildered and said, "You don't know, do you?"

"We will be getting to all that Coli. You coming later?" Auntie Eva asked.

"Yeah, I'll be there." Mrs. Colibri said with a smirk.

Suddenly a jovial Black man bellowed, "There is my favorite spirit body! Hey Eva!"

Eva turned around and rolled her eyes then said, "Clarence. What do you want Clarence?"

Clarence embraced my auntie and kissed both her cheeks as she winced with each one; then looked him up and down and smirked.

I interjected, "So how do you two know each other?"

Clarence chuckled and said, "Oh, we know each other. I mean we know each other, biblically. I could never get off your horse, girl."

"Why are you so nasty?! She doesn't need to know all that!" Auntie screeched

"Now I wanna know," I said as I folded my arms and switched my hip with an attitude.

Auntie Eva sighed and explained, "Back in the day I was a little free. Let's just say that. And my mama didn't like it, but I loved being a vibrant free woman who loved many men. It wasn't for nothing. I was the dumping ground for men's problems with their work and wives. No one ratted me out because I had so many secrets that I could have whatever I wanted. Not bad for a colored woman in the '30s. But ego is a helluva thing..."

Clarence interjected, "Yeah, your *hoespionage* caught up to you."

Auntie shouted, "Shut up!" Then continued, "I finally met someone I loved, and we got married and had a few kids. James Thomas. But when my previous lovers found out they got jealous and feared I was sharing their business secrets. So, they shot me. Clarence was the only one not to retaliate. We actually became good friends, although he wanted more. He tried to stop the men who came for me but instead witnessed my murder, felt guilty, and died of a heart attack shortly after. We both ended up on the horse for a while."

A jolly red-haired, freckle-face, chubby Irish woman ran up to Ife and hugged her. Ife hugged her back tightly. The Irish woman jumped into Clarence's arms as he swung her around. Then the woman hopped on me and gave me a hug and kiss on the cheek! I backed up and said sternly,

"Who are you, white woman?"

"Oh angel, you don't know do you?" the Irish woman replied

Auntie Eva clapped her hands together and said, "Aht, Aht, Aine! She will know in due course. Aine and I have a lot in common is all."

"Ceart go leor! You ready for the party?!" Aine asked excitedly.

"Yes! And I can't wait to change into my new..." Auntie's excitement stopped as she stared ahead at a man dressed in all black with cinnamon skin and dark eyes.

He gracefully navigated the crowd rocking his muscular shoulders back and forth as he marched towards us. Auntie began to shake in fury as he inched his way into our circle. He slyly smiled and said,

"Good evening everyone. Eva."

"You stay the hell away from me." Eva growled through clenched teeth.

He blew a kiss at her and said, "Is that any way to treat an old friend. Get off the horse baby. You spirits have a good evening," He turned and looked at me charmingly, "You too, Felicia."

Auntie Eva lunged at him as the cinnamon man smoothly avoided her and walked away. Clarence and Aine held Eva back and started whispering in her ear to calm her down. She shuttered and took deep breaths until she calmed down. She closed her eyes, shed one tear, and motioned to everyone that she was alright. I put my arm around her and whispered,

"Auntie, are you alright?"

She turned and smirked at me and said, "Don't worry about me, baby. I just don't like 'em because they twelve generations deep of ain't shit!"

"Eva! Do you want to go back on the horse again! You were just able to get off not long ago." Clarence shouted.

"Clarence does have a point, Ife. There is only so much of a grudge you can hold before you're back in the well," Aine added.

"Well, it's the damn truth. The Atawitam and Lolonyo tribes are causing all kinds of havoc to men and women. I swear those families were born from a bad seed that just keeps blooming like a weed no matter what anyone do. How you have destructive people generation after generation? That's not how they're blessed up!" Auntie ranted.

Suddenly a burst of melodies rang through the tent and all the spirit bodies cheered, outshining the music being played. Everyone started to scuttle towards the bright orange exit tunnels as their clothes began to transform on them. Shoes melted away revealing shadow-like feet illuminated in body paint. The shadows continued up their legs changing the style of their clothes and hair revealing shades of glowing pink, blue, yellow, red and green over a shadowed body.

The bass of drums and techno sounding melodies started to take over the glowing tunnel. Eva sashayed in front of me as the shadow and colors transformed her simple shoes to six-inch heels, and her skirt into a black leather pant suit that gracefully shimmied up her body. As we neared the exit, the shadow and lights started to braid the back of hair up to a high-top double bun with swirls of color through her curls. As we emerged out of the tunnel Eva turned around revealing completely black skin with pink circles around her glowing golden eyes, yellow lips, and bright blue tribal marks on the side of her face. She gleamed and shouted,

"Today we celebrate the new beginnings, baby girl! This is our harvest day celebration."

"Your what?!" I exclaimed

Auntie laughed and grabbed a hold of my hand and began to dance trying to make me relax. She laughed, as she realized I was very confused. Then she clapped her hands together and then elegantly lifted them as my prison wardrobe began to sparkle and turn into glowing gold peep-toe boots, a gold fluffy cocktail dress, and flecks of gold paint all over my face and body. We both gleamed and started dancing to the escalating beat. All of the spirit bodies danced together in harmonious joy in various dance styles through their different spirits generations. We danced for hours under the stars; stars that reflected the glowing paint on everyone's skin causing the entire area to look like the break of dawn.

Aine and Mrs. Colibri joined us gleefully trying to teach me their dances. Mrs. Colibri had on a pink, green, and yellow silk halter floor length dress. Her long wavy hair was covered in jewels that twinkled as she whipped her hair around her glowing blue eyes. Aine had on a blue cocktail style dress bedazzled in green jewels that matched her glowing green eyes and blue jewels in her hair that was braided back into an elegant bun.

We all danced together for two hours before two women in golden masks and decorated hair joined us. They grabbed my hands and forced me into a circle with them as we all danced together with Ife, Aine, and Mrs. Colibri all surrounding us. I had never felt so free in my life. There was no pain, no worries, no drama, it was...heaven.

A man with green hair and yellow eyes grabbed a microphone and bellowed, "From the source, to the soil, to the stars we..." He pointed the microphone to the crowd as they shouted,

"MANIFEST!"

Suddenly all the men surrounded all the female spirits and were doing a combination of traditional celebratory dances and breakdancing; stomping their feet and twisting their bodies in so many ways. All of the women gathered in the center, continuing to do their dances. Then suddenly a whistle came over the crowd stunning them to silence. The beat slowly started to pick up again as all the men linked arms and started murmuring 'Manifest' in their own tribal and earthly tongues. Then a woman let out a war cry and the rest of the women let out their respective battle cries and everyone started jumping up and down as the beat dropped again! We danced and jumped and screamed and praised until it was almost sunrise.

~

The party simmered down and the spirits dispersed. We walked through a field as the sun began to rise. The teal starlight sky had a rainbow arched across all of Tribeland that slowly leaked out an array of pink, blue, yellow, and green light. Ife hooked my arm and we walked away from the dwindling party and the horse merry-go-round slowed as the horses and riders slowly disappeared. As we got further away from the carnival Ife's outfit changed back to simple low-heeled shoes, a white cotton dress, and her hair unraveled to show her bouncy curls that cascaded down her back.

"I've been here a while." I blurted out.

"Yeah, almost eight hours." Eva said.

"Eight hours! I gotta get back or I'm going to miss breakfast!"

"In the pen?!" She laughed "Were you looking forward to dry toasted bagels, baby girl?!"

We laughed and she continued, "Relax; it's eight Tribleland hours, which is about twenty-four minutes in earth time. Come on, suga."

We continued forward. She was curiously quiet and kept smiling at me as we walked through the increasingly thick tall grass. There were abrupt chirp-like whispers coming from the distance and I started to see women dressed in white kneeling down talking to glowing budding flowers. We walked through the rows of women and a melodic humming sound got louder as we walked through the rising jungle like grass.

We arrived at a vast field of sunflowers that nearly towered over us. Eva kept walking forward with an elegant stomp through the dirt. The center of the sunflowers twinkled in flecks of blue and green light with songs being sung from them and the petals hummed rainbow vibrations. As we approached a hill she annoyingly grunted, lifted her skirt, kicked off her shoes, marched forward and ordered,

"Pick those up for me."

I picked up the shoes and chased her up the hill. As I tried to catch my breath I shouted, "Auntie! What is this place?"

Eva snapped her head around looking confused and lifted her arms and said, "What's it look like? It's a field of sunflowers!"

She continued forward, fussing inaudibly. I shrugged and as I took another step another black woman jumped out of the sunflower stems and smiled at me. She kept smiling at me with a bright light in her eyes and familiar smile. She was dressed in a colorful skirt and loose white top. She began to twirl around me smiling and laughing. She began dancing with moves from every era. She did a big spin and lifted her arms with glee as she finished. Finally, she stopped and hugged me and said,

"Thank you for loving her. Having you made my little Jasmine so happy and strong. All of us could not stop dancing whenever you were around. Her love for you charged her spirit up so much that we could all feel it. You are a part of her breaking her own curses and we are so happy to have you here. Daughter. You tell my little Jasmine we, Raha, are always watching out for her...and you."

She released me from her loving embrace and I quivered with tears. As she wiped them Raha said, "You should hurry. Your Auntie is a lovely, but impatient woman."

"Lil' girl!" Eva bellowed from the top of the hill.

I ran up the hill and saw Eva standing in a small dirt circle amid the field of sunflowers. She had her hand on her hips with a stern look, then she released a smile. She lowered her arms and gracefully clasped her hands together and said,

"Do you know where you are?"

I hesitated, "Uh, a sunflower field.

"That it is," she chuckled. "This is where we harvest new souls to be sent to earth for whatever their divine assignments are. In each of these flowers are 100 souls all nurtured by the mothers of Tribeland. These harvesting fields are across Tribeland. This plot of flowers though, this is for the little Black babies. Baby, this is where you were born. Can you hear them?"

I shrugged and said, "I hear voices, yes. But, I've seen a lot of other weird shit already. Why not add voices in my head?"

Ife laughed and nodding in agreement, she walked towards me, gracefully took me by the hand and sat us both down in the circle. She played with the rich black soil with her feet as she explained that the Source plants seeds in the soil. Then a mother from every type of tribe would come to a section and bless the babies with spiritual gifts, prayers, and stories. As they grow these things become a part of their soul and it translates in their human form. She laughed at my process from shock to figuring out how souls work. I exclaimed,

"Is that why so many Black people like anime? Someone came here and whispered it in their soul?! "

"Something like that. Or if a baby is both Black and whatever else, the mothers here had already blessed such a soul to be created. We are assigned sections by the Source and go to the flowers as directed and raise these babies," Eva explained, then cupped my face and continued,

"Many children are born from the same roots, harvest, or share the same spiritual mother and sometimes meet again in life as family, lovers, neighbors, and friends. Ya know how sometimes, you meet people and you just click? It's because you were raised here together first. Those are usually the folks that stick around till ya'll come back here."

"Jasmine is my sunflower sister?" I asked

"There ya go!" Auntie playfully popped my shoulder then said, "Ya got it! Today is harvesting day. All the Black mothers are going to come here soon and bless our babies one last time before we return them to God's hands and plan."

"Hold up." I paused. "What about miscarried or aborted babies. Is that just a waste of the soul?"

Eva preached, "Uh, uh honey. God don't waste no souls. He will send them right back where they belong no matter what anyone does to them. Whether that is on the parents or on them. And if they can't get right by choice, they pass a better chance down the bloodline and hop on the horse until their soul is settled."

"Wow. Hold up, are you sending me back as a baby or something?! Oh no. Oh no, Auntie please don't make me go through puberty again!" I panicked.

"Girl, hush! Not quite. I am sending you back, but there is someone here that wants to bless your journey." Eva stated

I heard a rustling behind us and jumped up to see Jasmine's ancestors, then another woman, and another emerged until we were completely surrounded. Ife stood up and walked to the center of the circle and smiled at me. She looked towards the falling rainbow and then spread her arms and a gospel and jazz style melody belted out of her,

From sacred roots you have been raised

Then the surrounding ladies sang,

To become a soul that does not wither when challenged

Being human is not a divine reward

You are a plan, to move the world forward.

Ha-ya. Ha-ya. E-ter-nal.

The ground began to quake around us and suddenly the circle started to spin around. The plots of sunflowers were all circulating around the center. The sky began to brighten as the colors washed away the night sky. The tribe mothers continued to sing in a beautiful fusion of gospel, classical, and jazzy voices.

Imperishable entity born from a marvelous

structure laced together within the starlight

the souls of the mothers have sung

divine one take your place in line

Ha-ya! Ha-ya!

Small flecks of light began to shine all over the center of the sunflower and worked its way out, shining brighter with each of the petals. Ife walked towards me and grasped my arms as she continued to sing along with the other mothers as the whipping wind carried their voices to the stars. Suddenly a prism of light overtook Ife's entire being. Then it began to reveal a woman in a white linen dress with smooth beautiful skin.

Ha-ya! Ha-ya!

Eternal ones, eternal ones

connect to your roots

The prism faded away up to her face as she continued to sing with the power of 10,000 souls. She looked in my eyes as she continued to sing the song and I couldn't speak. *Bev- Mommy?*

the truth

of your light

the power of your bloodline

Ha-ya Ha-ya Ha-ya!

An electrifying light overtook the crops and flashed upward then I was back in my cell and awakened with my cell mate standing over me. I jumped up from the bed, ready to fight. She backed up and laughed then said,

"This lady just dropped this off for you."

My cellmate handed me a letter and shuffled back up to her bunk. I opened a small letter. It was from Jasmine!

Felicia, if you were going to rob a place you could've gone to Saks. Hang in there, things will always get better. And at the bottom of the letter, she had drawn a sunflower with a message: ***We're all praying for you.***

NOT BROKEN, JUST BROKE

When we break, we breakthrough...supposedly

∿∿∿. ∿∿∿

ON THE THIRTEENTH day, I went to court. The moment the court officer called my name, I stood up with the handcuffs around my wrists. No one was in the courtroom on my behalf to speak for me. As the judge began talking, I turned around and in walks my social worker, independent living coordinator and foster mother Kima. I thought that no one was coming to support me. In fact, I felt that they were more disappointed in me than I was in myself.

When I turned back around my heart was at ease. The weight I had in my heart had lifted and I knew that I would soon be ok. When the judge began to speak to me, I had no words for him.

The Judge stated "Young lady, you should be ashamed of yourself. You are going to the number one international criminal justice school and you are out in the world committing criminal activity. You have your foster care agency here and your foster mother in your corner advocating for you and how great of a youth you are. Make this the final and last time I see your face. The next time, you will be sentenced to jail time."

I am adjudicating you as a youthful offender and you will be sentenced to three years' probation. "Upon completion of your probation, your record will be sealed. Take this as a lesson learned and do something with your life". When the judge rendered his decision to release me, I looked at him and felt a sudden relief. I walked out of that courtroom and knew that next time I wouldn't be so lucky. I walked out of that courtroom relieved that I got a second chance. Was it God? Was it Ife? Was it the judge's kind heart? Who knows? But I knew that I had to create something new in my life.

∽

Learning to accept full responsibility for my own actions was key for me to move forward. Taking responsibility reminded me that I was human and still needed to learn along the way. Having made so many mistakes gave me the real-life experience needed. Being incarcerated for those thirteen days was a lesson I needed to be taught so that I could see where I didn't want to be.

While receiving counseling during my childhood, I can remember when a psychologist told me that *"the older we become as people, our experiences and the wisdom gained is what helps us to become tolerable and see how and why things played out the way they did."* The wisdom I had gained gave me the opportunity to take responsibility for my actions and analyze life from the lens of what I could do better moving forward.

Laughing was something that became front and center in life for me. It helped me to live stress-free, to be in the moment, and to find rehabilitation in overcoming some of the adversities I was facing. I learned to laugh about the things that would annoy most people. I saw that it was easier to laugh than to get angry and waste my energy on something that would give me nothing but grief. Additionally, I incorporated daily self-talks regarding what I expected from myself. Broadening my horizon meant that

I would need to take risks. It was all or nothing and I chose to go for it all. But first I had to get a job that would hire someone on probation. So, that meant a burger spot run by the most ornery man I had ever met in my life. If you were sick, if you had a death in the family, or were running five minutes late you became worthless to him. I kept my head down most of the time and did my job.

It was what I had so that is what I worked with. I cleaned the counters and grills everyday while some of my co-workers laughed it up in the back. They never got in trouble but if I looked in their direction the owner would appear in my face and point for me to get back to work. It was hard to stay focused some days, but I would go to a prayer group at my church led by the first lady. I was surrounded by women that had gone through life making a ton of mistakes.

Regardless of what they had done or been through they would talk about their pain, speak their truth and allow what they have been through to influence others. These beautiful women weren't worried about how people would look at them. They were gracefully broken women striving to do better. They were challenging themselves and pushing through life correcting mistakes that God has given them a chance to make right. They'd always say, *"God will allow you to go through things to make you stronger and give you a chance to grow. He helped me walk into my talents and the purpose He had on my life."*

So, one spring day I took a chance.

A lady in a dark purple dress and suit jacket walked into the burger place one day and placed a massive order for an office party. I took the order of 25 burger combinations that all had specific instructions like I was taking roll at school. The woman was impressed and cheerily said,

"I think you're really smart. You don't need to be behind these counters. You need to be selling luxury!"

She insisted I take her card and come to the next meeting they were having at an office in downtown Brooklyn. Then she happily scuttled her way out of the restaurant. One of the guys from the back walked up behind me and said,

"You're not going to go to that bullshit meeting, are you?"

"It sounds like a better opportunity than here," I replied.

"Tell you what, I'll go with you and if it's a good opportunity then *you* can take me on a date."

"What?! Dude I don't even know you!" I exclaimed

"I'm Reggie, your shift manager, remember?" Reggie stated with a smile.

I looked him up and down trying not to show my admiration for his lean yet muscular physique, looking like he was chiseled out of a coffee bean, with a grin that could turn a nun into a sinner, and eyes that could capture your soul. I couldn't breathe as I studied his movements that made it seem like he was posing for GQ magazine. My gaze was interrupted by him speaking,

"Felicia."

"Huh?" I answered.

"That's your name, right? Felicia?" Reggie asked.

"Y-yeah it is," I fumbled.

"Ok, well look, we don't have to go to that meeting if you don't want to. We can just go out. I know you're a workaholic and need a break," Reggie said with a charming smile.

"You know what, sure." I responded with a smile.

"Ok I'll switch your shift on Friday, so you'll be free. And, uh, I'll pick you up at 5:30." He was grinning from ear to ear.

I was counting the days all week, anxiously picking out an outfit every day and acting out how I would play coy on this non-date. While we were at work, I was all smiles and giggles at every joke. On Thursday, before he went home for the night we were talking about the injustices within the Black community and family and I blurted out,

"I know all about it, I'm a foster kid."

Reggie stopped in his tracks and raised an eyebrow. All I thought was *"Shit, now he's going to think I'm some freak, broken, foster kid and he won't want to go out with me."* But then he said,

"Wow. I'm really sorry you had to go through that. It doesn't define you though. I'll see you tomorrow." He grinned and walked away.

My heart stopped and I was entranced by his gracious encouragement and smile. Finally, someone who didn't see me as a case number or my story. I was just me.

Entranced or not I didn't want Reggie to know where I lived yet, so I gave him the address to Sis' building. I rummaged through all the outfits I had picked out all week and threw all of them on the floor and finally settled on to some jeans, a crop top, and some short boots. I ran to the elevator and hurried to wait for him in front of the building. Then he pulled up on a moped.

"Um, where are we going?" I asked looking him up and down confused.

"To chase the moon baby," He said with a smile.

"To do what now? I am not dressed to hop on a bike!" I protested.

"It's not a bike, it's a moped. I thought the motorcycle would be too fast so I rode this over. It's better than taking the train."

"But where are we going on this motorbike thing?"

"To, chase, the moon. Do you trust me?" Reggie asked and I nodded.

"Hop on we have a long ride ahead, and it may be a little bumpy, but it'll be fun."

I thought about the car ride when Illeri was trying to get me to let go and trust. All I could see was her hair blowing in the wind and the smile on her face. Maybe that was my ancestor's way of telling me to enjoy the ride of life. So, I shrugged and damn near skipped my way over to the moped. He gave me a helmet, told me to hold on and we pulled off.

Next thing I knew we were crossing the Williamsburg bridge and the sun was starting to set. The sky was painted in orange, red, and pink as the stars began to slowly play peek-a-boo through the receding colors. I laid my head on Reggie's back and watched the last bit of sunlight skip across the river and took a deep breath of appreciation for its beauty. Reggie yelled,

"Let go and feel the air!"

"What?! Are you nuts I'll fall!" I screamed back

Reggie laughed, "Hold on to me with your thighs, stick your hands out and let it be. Stop holding on to fear sweetie."

I was terrified. But I kept thinking about how Illeri trusted Chike. We took off over that cliff. As I scooted closer and my thighs clenched on to his I slowly let go and allowed the air to take my arms back. It was the most dangerous and exhilarating experience so far. We made our way through Manhattan. I'd let go at different moments as the sun ran away from the rising moon. We finally pulled over in Harlem to park. He helped me off the bike.

"You enjoy the ride?" He asked with a big smile.

"That was some scary shit, but amazing." I replied.

We walked into a lounge that was so dimly lit it was hard to see where to walk. The stage was lit enough to help guide the way. A jazz band played as a waitress that blended in with the shadows sat us down and gave us menus. Reggie told me that this spot hosts poetry and jazz nights on Fridays and he wanted to start our night off opening our souls a little bit.

'Coming to the stage our mistress of the soul, Madam Rae!' The host announced.

The crowd clapped and cheered as an Afrocentric woman gracefully came to the stage and bowed to the left and right and blew kisses.

"I'm not gonna be up here too long ya'll. I just want to say a little something that's on my heart."

Black child, canvas for stars to shine on why don't you love thyself?

Shall I preach? Shall I teach?

Or will you look within to see the magic of your skin.

Black child, Black as the roads adventures travel on.

Black as the ink that creates nations.

Black as the sky when it creates storms that shifts all courses and actions.

Black child you are the beginning and end of creation.

When the world wants something new, it starts with you.

By the might of your imagination or the laborer of change.

Black child, shall I teach? Shall I preach?

Or will look within and see that your magic is not a sin.

The crowd roared with excitement and stood to their feet in applause. She graciously smiled and blew kisses to everyone, then she stared directly at me. Reggie excused himself to go to the bathroom. I watched him walk away, enamored with his swag. When I turned back around Madam Rae was in my face.

"Hey, suga." Madam Rae said in a sultry voice. I was so taken by her appearance and graceful power that I couldn't speak. She smiled and said, "Baby, what you doing here with trouble?"

"What do you mean?" I asked.

"You're pretty young, aren't you beautiful? I could be wrong. But just remember your worth," Madam Rae said, and she gracefully walked away.

Reggie came back and we continued on with our date. We ate, tossed back a few, and laughed about work, and other "Brooklynisms". We left out of the lounge and Madam Rae was standing outside smoking. She looked at me again and mouthed, *"stay out of trouble."* We hopped back on the moped and took off into the city. We rode west towards the Hudson and then back towards Central Park and pulled over to dance to street musicians. We rode up to the upper east side and back down to the lower east side enjoying the views of the New York City in the spring. We went back across the bridge to Brooklyn and I stretched my arms out again feeling the night air and embracing life. He took us all the way to Prospect Park. We parked and started walking.

"Um, are you sure we can be here right now?" I asked.

"Maybe," Reggie chuckled. "Probably not, but it's ok if the cops catch us; we can act like ignorant tourists wandering in Brooklyn."

"You're so silly. My accent is so thick they'd never believe it," I laughed.

"Leave it to me. 'Beggunyapardon sir, but we are coming way up from the nation of Texas and are just taking in the sites of this here fine park. We be fittin' to leave though if that'll suit.' Reggie said this in the thickest southern accent I've ever heard.

I burst into laughter, "That'll work."

"You know, I was debating if I would share this or not. But since you shared a little bit about your past, I thought I'd let you know that you weren't alone." Reggie stated.

"What do you mean?" I asked

Reggie took a deep sigh and said, "You were talking about foster care yesterday. I have parents, but I might as well have been a foster kid. My Dad used me when I was small to attract his side pieces, then when I got older I was the lookout to make sure nobody around the way caught him. He'd call me a good son for keeping his secrets, but my Moms knew. Then with her, I swear she arrived on this planet angry as hell. If she wasn't yelling at me or beating me for something she thought I did, she was making me a cake and calling me the best son in the world."

"Oh my God, that is really emotionally abusive."

" I know it's not *foster care* but it is a broken family. I've never really known what love looks like or what a home was supposed to look like. When I turned 18, my auntie Irie, took me in and told me I could stay for however long I wanted. So that's where I'm at now," he explained.

"I've known love as far as what a mother could be, but it still wasn't my own. I'm sorry your parents treated you like a chess pawn." I said this to comfort him.

"Eh, it's cool. People do things and we have to forgive them. Life is short. What do you want out of life?" Reggie asked.

"I want a successful career and a family."

"Oh, ok. Well, I'm sure you can have those things. You have fun tonight?"

"Yeah!"

"You think we can chase the moon again sometime soon?"

I smiled and he grinned and inched closer to me. *Oh my God this was it. He was going to kiss me. Shit, is my breath fresh?* is all I was thinking. He kissed my forehead and picked a flower that dangled from a branch and handed it to me. I giggled and took the flower. We got lost in each other's eyes and then finally the real thing, a kiss that warmed me from the soles of my feet to the pit of my soul and sent waves of energy through my body.

Over the next few weeks, we would sneak kisses at work, go out on chasing moon dates or simple ones at restaurants, movies, and long walks through Brooklyn. He would spout so many philosophies on life about how we must take charge of our destiny and not allow anyone to derail us. He wanted to get into property management and flip houses so that he could create generational wealth. Finally, someone who thought like I did! One night he brought me a rose and bopped me on the nose with it and said,

"Felicia, I can't believe I'm saying this but I love you."

I gushed uncontrollably and shouted, "I love you too!"

The next week our mean-ass manager found out that we were dating and berated me about it calling me a Jezebel and I should be ashamed of myself. He didn't say a word to Reggie. Despite Reggie trying to stick up for me, the manager fired me. I marched out of the restaurant gladly because I didn't want the job anyway. Reggie chased after me and apologized profusely for what happened. I shrugged it off and he grabbed me and kissed me then said,

"Hey what are you doing this weekend?"

"Looking for a job I guess. Maybe I can check out that purple suit lady gig" I chuckled

Reggie laughed, "Aw, hell nah. Well, it's my aunt Irie's birthday, and I really want you to meet her.

"Okay!" I yelped enthusiastically

The weekend came and he picked me up on his moped and we rode over to his aunt's house in Crown Heights. I was so nervous to meet her because this was the woman he held in such high regard. He gleefully swung open the door and reggae and the smell of spices blasted out of the house and then he shouted,

"Wha gwaan family!"

"Ayyye!" The family shouted back.

His cousin ran up to us and she yelled, "Reg-i-nald, we see your ugly ass all the time! Who dis?"

I laughed, and he presented me to her, "Gabi this is my love, Felicia."

"Love! Auntie, Reggie in love! Did you know?" Gabi yelled. Then she grabbed my hand and pulled me with her, "Come on, Miss Love!"

Reggie laughed and walked over to his other cousins as I was brought to the kitchen table where his aunt sat surrounded by other female family members. She was a plump woman who was using a cane and had short dreadlocks. I smiled and nearly curtsied and said,

"Hi Mrs. Irie, I'm Felicia."

She laughed and said, "I know who you are baby. My Reggie has told me all about you. Y'all clear out of here I want to talk to this one."

Everyone but Gabi left and Aunt Irie took my hands and looked at me with pure endearment, then she snapped her head at Gabi and said, "I said everybody get out!"

"Nah Auntie I want to talk to this one too!" Gabi insisted.

We chatted about my past and they were both enthralled about my journey so far. Gabi was talking more about the family and how Reggie's mother is their direct family and his father was a guy she met around the way in Brooklyn. Aunt Irie went on to say that the women in the family are dedicated to their men to a fault. She explained that she had to use a cane now because of a man she loved. The weight of the world was so heavy on his back that he had to take it out on her sometimes. Other times he would seek comfort with other women. But she understood because men have a hard time in the world and no one to turn to but their women. It's an honor to take the pain because that means you are trustworthy enough to bear it. That is an exalted place.

"If he hit you, it don't matter unless it bruises. If he falls into some other pussy it doesn't matter if he doesn't love her. He's a hurt boy and he needs you to be patient with him, because this world isn't. He's a good boy. And will be an incredible man someday if you just give him a chance. Alright, baby?"

Gabi interjected, "Hell I'm miserable with my husband and I'm miserable without him. We some miserable motherfuckas but we love each other. That just how it go."

I was highly confused, but it made me wonder if my mother had worked harder to make my father happy would they have fallen into the drug habit that ended up taking both of them out? We kept chatting and laughing at family members unable to dance and looking at photos of people who had passed on. Suddenly I saw a woman with a cobra tattoo walk over to Reggie and start flirting with him. She caressed his face and he took her hand and danced with her. I was enraged and got up to go address both of them, then Gabi grabbed my arm and said,

"Don't worry about her boo. She's the community ho. She's a right-of-passage pussy that almost everybody has had. Her Mama a ho, her gran a ho; they several generations of hoes screwing everyone in Crown Heights. She don't mean nothing to him and is just tempting him. Leave it be."

I watched them dance together for twenty minutes and kept shaking in fury and Gabi stroked my arm to calm me down. The community hoe eventually left and Reggie came and grabbed me from the kitchen. I tried to hide my anger and it became easier as he danced with me and was incredibly affectionate with me for the whole family to see. The party went into the night and Reggie started to kiss me like he was making up for our lost time together of years passed.

We glided up the stairs to his room and he swept me up in his arms and carried me across the threshold. He kicked the door closed behind us and slid me onto the bed. He adored my lips then my neck, then my breasts, my stomach, and finally showed his appreciation to my womanhood. While I quivered with the sensation of being drunk, high, and electrified he kept whispering *'Do you like it, do you want more? Or do you want me?* To which I replied, '*All three!*' He climbed on top of me and when we connected my body exploded in warmth, pain, and I moaned as I welcomed him in. We shook the bed as we were intertwined on top, on the side, upside down with the beat of his grunts and the melody of my moans being a soundtrack of something I thought I'd never have, love. Finally, we looked in each other's eyes and exploded once more; we wore out our bodies and slipped into a coma-like state.

Around 3:30 in the morning my eyes shot open and I thought about how complicated love and life could be. They didn't discuss relationships when we're talking to social workers. I started to reflect on when I was about to leave Little Flower Family and Children Services in Jamaica Queens. I went down a rabbit hole of memories that made me think about how much I was and was not prepared to go after what I really wanted.

I never mapped out a plan on what I needed to do while in foster care that would help me prepare for the real world. Once I realized that my goal was no longer adoption at the age of 12, I began attending classes at my agency. Workshops were held every Saturday in the morning for youth that had a goal to live independently and succeed in adulthood. The workshops included everything from food preparation, to money management, housing, and education just to name a few.

These workshops were tailored to give me and other youth the foundation of what responsibility looked like in these areas, but, never really elaborated on what we needed to do more in depth and how to apply it to the different areas of our lives in which we could benefit. From the age of twelve until eighteen, Saturday workshops were the norm for me. Like many of the youth that attended these workshops, I was lost, confused, scared to do and want different, and often ashamed at the fact that I was another written off number in the system. Fortunately, for me, my Independent Living Coordinator often reminded me of why I needed to take these workshops seriously and encouraged me to continue to learn from them and seek additional knowledge outside of my foster care agency. From that moment, I began to realize that she wanted me to succeed. She saw something in me that I couldn't even see in myself.

One afternoon when I got out of school, I took the bus to Jamaica Avenue and met her. On my way to meet her, I kept asking myself, *What do you see yourself doing with your life once you age out?* Shockingly, I couldn't answer my own question. I remember standing by the back door of the Q56 bus, lost in my own thoughts and translation of what I thought I knew. This was mind blowing. Any other time I had the answers for my life. At least, I thought I did. As I stood there and stared in a daze, I knew that I needed to set a plan in motion so that I wouldn't subject myself to be the next homeless, incarcerated and uneducated foster youth. When I reached my stop and got off the bus on Jamaica Avenue, I remained clueless.

As I approached the doorway of where my Independent Living Coordinator was located, I lifted my head up with a smile. See, there were many different things I thought I knew I wanted for my life, but I really didn't have a clue about where I was going.

When I approached the doorway of the Coordinator's office, I pushed the door open and said," I got it. I know what I need to do to make sure that I am successful beyond foster care."

She looked up at me and said, "Huh? What are you talking about Felicia?".

"You once asked me what my intentions were once I left foster care, right?"

"Yes."

"Well, I plan on staying with Mrs. Roberts, if she lets me."

"Do you think that she will let you?"

"I believe she will," I responded.

"Well then that's good. Ask her and see what she says," She replied.

Sitting down at the desk in front of the coordinator, I pulled out my notepad and my pen and began writing down my goals one by one. Even if I didn't have all my thoughts together, I wrote down what I wanted. Setting such goals aligned me with what I needed to do for the time being and for the future to come. In setting goals, both short and long term, it helped me focus on achieving every task in order. Goals helped me with direction and destiny. One of the best things I learned was that when goals are implemented, written down and visible to see, it provides a clear focus on what's important and how to prioritize. Next, it gave me the chance to envision where I saw myself in three, five and even ten years. Creating goals gave me the ability to be creative and find different paths and directions to achieve them. Implementing goals has helped me to open the lines of communication for myself and anyone guiding me on my journey. Open lines of communication allow people the chance to offer you support where they can be of assistance.

But there I lay still wondering what was next. Who can I turn to that will guide me into the next phase? I got up to go to the bathroom. When I was washing my hands the mirror cabinet slipped opened and I saw all the different pills that Auntie Irie had to take because of her pain. I wondered, is a man worth all of this pain? Maybe she just didn't do it right. I closed the mirror door and when I looked in the mirror I jumped because my face was not mine! It was my Aunt Eva scowling at me and she yelled, *'What are you doing?!'* Then she disappeared. I opened and closed the mirror door repeatedly to see if the dick made me hallucinate. *Shit.*

The following week I received an eviction notice at my apartment and with no job or job prospects I didn't know what

I was going to do. I came by my old job and told Reggie what happened. He kissed my cheek in reassurance and told me I could live with him. I moved in with him and would make breakfast for him every morning then hit the pavement looking for work any, and everywhere. The economy was spiraling downward, and jobs were no longer aplenty. But Reggie and Aunt Irie loved having me in their home. One day I brought Reggie lunch at work and my old evil boss started cussing me out again. Reggie finally had it.

"You know what! I'm sick of your shit! I quit! You're not going to disrespect me or my woman and think I'm still going to work here! You don't pay me that much!" Reggie yelled, then picked up some saltshakers and threw them at him.

This enraged my old boss and he started yelling and chasing us out the door. Reggie and I sprinted down the street together as that very angry Armenian shouted and charged after us. His weight reminded him that he couldn't chase us, and he stumbled to a stop, but we kept running and laughing. I saw a smile on Reggie's face that I had never seen before. His rebellion brought him joy.

After we walked home, he got a text from a friend of his to come by and kick back in the rich part of Brooklyn. We hopped on the train and rode a while, making out and playing around to the annoyance, and adoration of onlookers. We hopped off and walked a few blocks then turned the corner and saw *mad people* swarming outside a brownstone blaring EDM music and lights. The cops were going to shut this party down for sure.

I quivered, "Reggie we better go. I don't think..."

"Trust me, we good. This is the only white boy I trust. Everyone who could complain about this party is at this party." Reggie laughed.

There were at least one-hundred people swarming in the streets cackling, screeching, and running around hugging each other like it was a family reunion. It seemed like every race that existed in New York City was at this party. I clung to Reggie as he looked around smiling and dapping up everyone he saw. Suddenly, I felt someone gently touch my arm and say,

"Don't be scared."

I turned around and saw a white girl with brown wavy hair and green eyes dressed in a Biggie shirt, blinking necklace, torn jeans, and black high-top sneakers. She smirked at me as we looked each other up and down. She continued in a calm, soulful tone,

"I'm Cara. Is this your first time at one of Mick's parties?"

"Yeah." I replied.

"They can get pretty wild. But you'll have a good time. Stick by me and I won't let anything happen to you." Cara said as she put a glowing neon necklace around my neck and smirked.

"Nah, I'm good. But thanks for the necklace," I said trying to get her to go away.

Reggie pulled me closer to him and glared at Cara. Cara looked at him and rolled her eyes and pursed her lips in annoyance. Then she turned to me and said,

"I'll find you inside, Felicia."

"How the hell you know my name?!" I shouted.

She disappeared into the crowd and I frantically tried to follow her, but Reggie pulled me close and whispered,

"Where you going?"

"That girl called me by my name, I don't know her! I need to..."

"Don't worry about her. She's just a weird white girl." He continued, "So, this guy hosts these parties all the time with over-the-top themes, or he just calls a bunch of people over and whatever happens, happens."

Suddenly a flamboyant white guy dressed in a neon green and purple top hat and long trench coat emerged from the house perched himself up on the railing, grabbed a bullhorn and bellowed,

"Welcome my darlings!"

The crowd cheered as he jumped down, spun around, jumped up onto the other railing with the assistance of another man dressed in a vibrant trench coat. He grabbed onto the crown molding around the doorway swaying around and, in his showman tone said,

"Tonight's theme is Wonderland! And I have got some *wooonders* for you! If you're new, welcome my darlings! If you're here again, you know the drill! Let's drink and be merry, cuz why?"

The whole crowd shouted in unison with him. "Imma lonely, rich, summabitch, and I'm ready to party!"

The man in the vibrant trench coat fired off a confetti cannon and the crowd scuttled up the steps cheering, screaming, and jumping around as we rushed inside. We were greeted by women scantily dressed in glitter bikinis and cat eye contacts, walking down the stairs with trays of ecstasy, blunts, cigars, and molly, while others ran through the crowd encouraging excitement around them. The lasers and neon lights made their bikinis twinkle; they looked almost...angelic. Mick started marching through the party with a gold, bedazzled drum major baton decorated in rapid blinking lights yelling, "Cheshire kitties here make your life pretty!"

Reggie uncontrollably grinned as the girls dispersed through the crowd. One made her way over to us. She smiled at me with both a menacing and friendly grin and pushed the tray towards me insisting I take something. I watched Reggie snatch up a cigar and another Cheshire kitty lit it for him. He took a puff and exhaled the smoke like a happy drug dealer and started dancing with the people around me.

I turned back around and all I could think about is, *"what if this is how it started with Bev? An innocent fix? A release."* As the party raged on around me, I suddenly couldn't hear anything and was focused on the tray and the smiling cat-eyed sparkle girl. I started to reach for the molly and then a Dominican chick grabbed my hand to dance as soon as the Biggie *Hypnotize* beat dropped.

"Come on Mami!"

She pulled me away from Reggie into the next crowded room where there wasn't much room to do anything except vibe to the music in a six-inch space. Cheshire kitties came around with shots of Patron and my new friend grabbed two and handed me one. We knocked them back and she smiled and said,

"You having fun Felicia?"

I stopped dancing and angrily said, "Who the hell are you? How do you know my name?"

She laughed, "I'm Jasmine's friend, Aura."

Just then Cara walked up and cheerily said, "You enjoying yourself?"

"Um, yeah." I hesitantly answered.

Cara called over one of the kitties to bring more shots, while I texted Jasmine.

"Jas, you know a Dominican chick named Aura."

Jasmine: Yeah, that's my girl! She hangs out with this dope-ass white girl a lot too. Cara.

How you know them?

Before she could answer Cara handed me another shot and rubbed my shoulder. She took her shot and smiled at me. Then grabbed another one and said,

"You don't want another shot? Come on it's a party."

"It's not that. How you know Jasmine?"

Cara excitedly said, "Jazzy! Oh, that's my girl! She and I met at.."

"Another party!" Aura interjected, "Not one of Mick's. We met a while back at a party we crashed and have been friends ever since. She's told us a lot about you."

"We recognized you from pictures. Sorry if I weirded you out earlier. I thought she might have told you about us," Cara winked and smiled, "Guess not. But no worries now we know each other."

Mick popped up behind us in a black cowboy hat, sunglasses, gold-painted chest, and flashing his fuchsia cape with a bedazzled bunny on it.

"Darlings! Less talkie, more dancie drinkie!" Mick spun around in his cape again, jumped in front of me, lowered his sunglasses, raised his eyebrow, and in an excited and intrigued tone said, "And you, chocolate darling, I have not seen you here before. Tell me, who has graced us with her presence?"

I giggled, "Felicia."

Mick swept his cape around his neck and said, "Brava! Welcome darling. Well, this is a house of healing. We remove bullshit from people's minds. So, tell me, what ails you? Why have you come to Monsieur Mick's?"

"Oh, me and my boyfriend came here. He finally quit his awful job and we came to celebrate." I explained.

He looked over both of my shoulders and then looked at me confused and asked, "I see no man flanked on your arm. Who is he?"

I started looking around for Reggie and saw him dancing with one of the Cheshire kitties. She grinded up on him while he smoked the last of his cigar with pure glee and grabbed her breasts. I started to march towards him and yoke that cat up by her neck and smack him with her. Aura and Cara grabbed my arms while Mick ran up to Reggie and shouted,

"Reggie you dastardly darling!"

Reggie stopped dancing with the kitty and dapped up Mick, "Eeeeeh! Great party as always!"

They continued to chat, and Cara pulled me by my hand away from them. We walked down to the basement that was in total blacklight with stripper poles everywhere and some people drunkenly dancing on the poles. We worked our way to the back of the room where there were giant pillows and hookahs. We sat down where a Japanese girl was laid back smoking the hookah and smiled as smoke escaped her mouth.

"Heeeey."

"Mai! Are you high?" Aura laughed

"Maybe I am, maybe I'm not. Maybe I'm here physically. Maybe I'm a figment of your imagination," Mai explained then took another puff.

"You high as shit," I laughed.

She laughed as smoke leaked out of her mouth once more, "That I am Felicia. Care to join me?"

"Um, do you know Jasmine too?" I asked

"Something like that. Did you two introduce yourselves?" Mai asked Aura and Cara.

"We wouldn't be sitting here if we didn't." Aura laughed

Mai got up from her comfortable pillows, extended her hand, and said, "Well, allow me to officially introduce myself. I'm Mai. I know you. I know them. I know Jas. And I know..."

"That she is incredibly high, but she wants to make a good impression, right?" Aura stated.

Mai laughed, "Si señora. You all had your fill or you wanna see what's upstairs? There's food up there."

"Your munchies-having-ass would know where the food is." Cara stated

"Let's take the elevator." Mai suggested.

We cut through the crowd of drunk people enamored with the people badly dancing on the poles and got on the private elevator. Mai went on to explain that she and Mick were adopted by an extremely wealthy couple that had very generous grandparents who died, leaving them full access to their trust funds. Mick truly is a lonely rich son-of-a-bitch that only started getting friends when he threw parties to make people feel good about themselves.

"His only happiness is based on how good he can make others feel, even if it's to forget the pain for a night. My brother means well, but he's lonely and lost." Mai explained. As we got off the elevator we entered on the master suite level.

The master suite was stark white. The walls were white with a black trim, there was a white sofa with a checkered table, white rugs, and black and white paintings. I was afraid to sit down; it looked like a museum. Mai walked over to a hidden refrigerator in the living room that opened up from the wall and grabbed a bowl of fruit and some bacon wrapped scallops and set it down on the table then plopped down on the couch. She gestured for us to have a seat and enjoy some food. Aura and Cara sat down, and I stood, too anxious to sit down.

"Do you live here too?" I asked.

"Sometimes. I go between the house in the Hamptons, my loft, and here." Mai explained, "So, what about you Felicia. We hardly know a thing about you accept that you're Jazzy's friend."

Oh my God, how was I going to explain that I am foster kid, jail bird, and broke trying to make it. I trembled with an incessant bumbling of uhs and ums. They all sat up waiting for me to speak. I took a breath and said,

"You know this has been an interesting and fun evening, but I think I should go. I don't really know Mick like that to be up in his bedroom."

I turned around to leave and Cara swiftly got up and stood in front me. I backed up away from her. While she had sympathetic eyes, I couldn't trust her. As I continued to back away, I bumped into Aura and jumped and stumbled away from her. Mai raised an eyebrow at me then looked at Aura and Cara. I ran away from them and hid in the bathroom.

I slammed the door closed and curled up on the floor. *How the hell did I end up here? Why did Reggie bring me here? These bitches are gonna do stuff to me. Windows? Windows? No windows! Dammit! How am I going to get out of here?* Suddenly, I heard whispers from outside the door. I slowly cracked the door open and saw Mai standing in front of a stand-up mirror, Aura was behind the mirror fixated on Mai and Cara was standing to the side talking to Mai.

"I told you I would look after her like we agreed on! It's not my fault if she's not ready to accept-please understand that we're all trying. She's just not ready yet. Even after everything else, I don't know if she'll ever be." Cara stated passionately.

Then Mai whispered in an airy voice, "Just be there for her. She has so much to learn."

I swung the door open and they all looked over to me. Cara started walking over to me and calmly said, "Hey sunshine. You feeling better? Looks like you had bit of an anxiety attack."

"A little bit yeah." I stated, "What's going on?"

"There is no easy way to say this." Cara began to explain.

"We knew about you through Jasmine, and she told us that if we ever crossed paths that we should look out for you." Aura interjected.

"We know that this is new for you. But I assure you that we mean no harm." Mai said to sooth me. "I think that you should come with us out to the house in the Hamptons and decompress a bit."

"I barely know you and I'm here with my boyfriend. He'll worry."

"Oh, your boyfriend that had his hand full of titty and hasn't looked for you in the last two hours? Yeah ok," Mai stated.

"Mai!" Cara and Aura shouted.

"I'm not going to lie to the girl! Come with us. He can find you tomorrow if he cares."

"He cares about me! He's just drunk!" I defensively explained. "And like I said, I don't know ya'll like that to be running off to your house."

Cara calmly walked over to me and embraced me. She held me with a familiar tightness that reminded me of how my favorite foster mother would. As she rubbed my back, I felt myself relaxing and collapsing on into the embrace. The other two surrounded me and Cara said,

"We were hoping you would be open enough to tell us but believe it or not we know your story. You're safe with us. Whenever you want to talk about it you can. But I really think you should come with us to the Hamptons."

HOLDING WATER // FELICIA R. WILSON

THE DOG & THE GOD

What good is magic?

What harm are lover's quarrels?

Neither are holy.

≈

WE LEFT THE master suite and took the elevator to the main floor where Mick had started an impromptu conga line. He was leading the front with his drum major baton, a velvet king crown on, black silk robe with his chest still glistening in gold body paint. He stabbed the ground with every step and stomped along yelling, *"Cha! Cha! Cha!"* with every boom of the stick as all the guests followed suit.

I tried to look for Derrick in the line but he was nowhere to be found in the crowd. Mai cackled and shook her head at her loony brother and waved us to the back to get to the garage. Aura and I slid into the back of Mai's Audi convertible and just as Cara was about to sit up front, Mai said,

"Felicia come sit up here with me."

Cara backed away from the door and presented the seat to me. I climbed into the front seat and Cara slid into the back, put on her seat belt and propped her feet up. We rolled out of the garage and drove through downtown Brooklyn, passing so many places through which I had to process my foster care experiences;. the child welfare court places where I had to meet counselors, and finally the corner where the homeless man said, "You're not a dog, you're a god."

As we got on 495 East, Mai put the top down and turned up the radio when the DJ spun in *DMX Party Up* everyone in the car went crazy. Mai was dancing and switching lanes and rapping the entire first verse adding her own sound effects so she wouldn't drop any N-bombs. Then she passed it to me and they were cheering me on then we all said, *I love my baby mama I never let her go!* We kept passing the mic rapping this song all the way down the highway. We kept dancing in the car to the mix on Hot 97, And then Cara had a strange request,

"Ayo Mai, tell Felicia the story about the soldiers."

Mai turned the radio down. "You want me to get deep after a turn up?"

"Why not? we'll be at your place in like 20 minutes anyway," Aura insisted.

Mai took a deep breath, looked at Cara and Aura in the rearview mirror, and began her story.

> *There were four soldiers that crossed paths in World War II in the South Pacific. There were three Americans, White, Black, and Latino and then a Japanese soldier. The Black and Latino soldiers were long-time friends that had rolled in with the Tuskegee Airmen in hopes of being equal afterwards, and the White Guy met up with them mid-battle. He wasn't*

thrilled about it, but they were fighting on his side. The Japanese soldier was fighting just to feed his family.

So, the three Johnny-Come-Latelys had wandered into the jungle delirious from fighting and fell asleep. The Japanese soldier wandered as well and stumbled upon the American soldiers. His training dictated that he kill them, but his heart could not kill sleeping men. So, he laid next to them. The Americans woke up and saw the Japanese solider. They pointed their guns at him and demanded he surrender. The Japanese soldier worked up the little English he knew to say, "Here for the money, not for the glory. Please brother." The Black and Latino soldiers lowered their weapons but not the White soldier. The White guy lowered his gun when he realized the soldier was being genuine. They all agreed that they were war dogs, they no longer had an identity. They all agreed that no matter what they felt personally, the world would select them to only be at war with each other. They had hoped that one day their descendants would be able to stop being war dogs.

The soldiers went their separate ways, had their families, but the war raged within them and they were never at peace. But one day their descendants found that peace and the war that the world placed upon the shoulders was finally over.

"Wow. So, what's the message of the story, love wins?" I asked.

Mai chuckled and said, "The point is, we are all tasked to carry burdens, even the ones we don't subscribe to. Our descendants should not be responsible to carry those burdens, but they are responsible to respect the war that was and stop it from happening again."

"It's interesting how you can't get it right, but your descendants can. Even if they don't know your whole story." Cara said.

"Our minds may not know the story, but our souls and our blood do." Aura said

I didn't want to tell them that I saw how stories are passed down from generation to generation. They already saw me freak out when they were only being nice to me. Although it was going to sound weird I wanted to contribute to this conversation. So, I blurted out,

"Maybe our ancestors speak to us in some kind of kamikaze way. Like a Mufasa situation." I laughed and awkwardly smiled.

Mai smiled; Aura gleamed; and Cara smirked and played with my hair and said,

"Maybe sweetie. Maybe they do."

We arrived at a house that backed up to a lake. It was a modern home with a completely white exterior but when we walked inside the vaulted ceilings were filled with paintings from every culture you could think, Where there were no paintings, the ceilings had reflective colorful paint. Before I could ask Mai laughed said,

"I know the house looks like an acid trip threw up in here. My darling brother wanted to paint the walls all neon and I refused, but his feelings were hurt so I got my art and he got to pick different walls to paint."

"Isn't this your house?" I chuckled and asked.

Mai hooked my arm and walked me further into her home and said, "Yes but when we received our inheritance he didn't want to separate at first, so we both lived here."

We ventured into the kitchen where Cara and Aura were eating on some snacks Mai left out. I walked over into the living room and saw photos of Mai and Mick as they were growing up. The one that struck me the most was the two of them in a black and white photo of them standing by the pool looking out to the sole sunbeam shining on them. Aura startled me when she threw a big bean bag pillow over the couch and it landed in front of me. She plopped down on it and said,

"Hey, Mai is making us some midnight snacks, you allergic to anything?"

I chuckled, "No."

"Hey Mai! Nothing you cook will kill her!" Aura shouted and we laughed.

I sat on the couch and said, "So this is all really hers huh?"

"Sure is!" Aura said jubilantly "What is your family like?"

"Honestly I'm still trying to get to know them. I'm a foster kid and a few months ago I was able to get in contact with some cousins," I said.

Cara sashayed over with a tray of turkey wraps and cheese and handed it to both of us, then said, "Well better late than never right? I was a foster kid too actually."

"Really?! Don't take offense, but you're White. You look like you come from some kind of money."

Everyone laughed and Cara started eating then continued, "Right you are sunshine. My mother had me when she was a teenager with her high school sweetheart. And oh, what a disgrace that was, so she left me at a child welfare office in her quaint little Connecticut town and got her life together. She married my father, went to school and became the suburban dream, but felt guilty about throwing me into the system. So, she found me when I was eight years old and brought me home."

"Did you hate her for that?" I asked.

Cara took a long gulp of her drink and then said, "I don't hate her per se. I hate that my grandparents made her feel unworthy and she cast that unworthiness unto me. And I spent my formative years feeling unworthy even when I got to be the suburban girl from Connecticut. I still ended up on the streets like they say foster kids do, because I felt unworthy."

Aura interjected, "That's around when I met her and she met her boo thang!"

"Ooooo, ok. What's his name?" I playfully asked.

Cara chuckled, "Her name is Prism. She really brought me into a place of worthiness and this hyper rabbit over here was too excited."

"Well yeah! Prism is amazing and I love to see amazing people get together and make magic out of madness. Life is hard you know." Aura stated.

"So, what about you two?" I asked pointing at Aura and Mai.

Mai cleared her throat and said, "I'm more focused on self-improvement and wellness than love these days."

"Honestly, I think that I was meant to be a nun, because I am so focused on my spiritual self that I don't make as much time for love." Aura stated.

Mai inched closer to me and nudged my shoulder then said, "So, what's the deal with your guy?"

"We're together and he's a little troubled but he needs me. Black men carry so much on their backs and it's up to us help them carry their load," I said.

Cara and Aura stared at me as they sipped their drinks and Mai put her arm around me and said, "A few years ago I gave my all to my first real love and he had a heavy load on him too. We had moved in together and were planning a future together. Then this woman who only satisfied his need to escape his reality caught his eye. He told me it was over and I fought tooth and nail to bring him back, degradingly so, and I slept with him to try and reconnect. He finished before I could even begin to get mine, got up, said thank you and walked out the door. Leaving all the pain he had transferred to me while not taking on any of mine. Be careful with who you think is worthy to carry burdens for. Odds are they are looking for a dumping ground, not a partner to help them build."

"You barely know me Mai! How dare you say that?!" I shouted.

Mai smirked and held me closer, "I know of your light as displayed by Jasmine. You're a fighter and since she loves you, we love you. Sisterhood is that simple. Every day we get to figure out why we love another woman so much and it's beautiful. I just don't want you to be consumed by the allure of what he could be instead of what he is."

"You never know, he could change and take charge over his issues," Aura said hopefully.

Cara changed the subject and we started talking about our craziest moments in the city. We danced and ate and drank way too much all night until we all passed out.

I walked outside as the sun was rising and found Cara standing by the infinity pool wrapped up in a green knit shawl and her clothes from the night before, smoking a blunt. She stared out into the nearby bay as if she was waiting for something. She turned around to look at me and blew out the smoke as the sun started to peak over the bay and twinkled in her seemingly honey-like eyes; which confused me because her eyes are green.

"You going to stand there and stare or did you want to ask me something?" Cara said.

"Um, well what are you doing up so early?" I asked.

"Talking to God." Cara said as she took another hit of her blunt and stuck it out to offer me some, "You want a hit?"

I shuttered, "Nah. I don't do drugs because..."

"Of your Mom I know. I know." Cara nodded and took another puff.

"How do you know so much about me?" I asked.

"Jazzy. I guess you're wondering why I am out here smoking a blunt and calling it prayer?" She asked, as I nodded. She continued, "I have anxiety and this keeps me calm. Are you also wondering why my eyes are brown and not green?"

I shrugged and said, "I figured you had contacts."

She chuckled, "Well that's a theory. My eyes change color. In the morning my eyes are my grandmother's and by the end of the day my mother's. Do your eyes change color? Is that a family trait?"

"No. Not to my knowledge. So, were you really praying?"

Cara dropped her blunt and smashed it into the grass and said, "Yup. I had to find myself. I had to find my inner god if I was going to make it. I went to church growing up as a good little Irish Catholic chillin' in elite suburbia of Connecticut. I had everything any kid could ask for. Good parents, good school and all and yet I felt so disconnected. So, I did the whole runaway, wild child, druggy bit for about two years. Come to find that is a family trait for lost souls. Then one day while I was laying like a dead dog in an alley I met Aura. She cleaned me up, introduced me to Prism who loved me in a way I had never known. Then they introduced me to Mai, who introduced me to God in a whole new way."

I was so confused and asked, "Cara if you had everything given to you how can you not feel connected to it. I would have killed to grow up in the suburbs instead of..."

"Running scared and angry to 50-11 homes when you were really running from the pain Bev left behind?" Cara interjected. I was taken aback by her statement but before I could inquire more she said, "Felicia, we met for a reason and I'm so glad I found you. Don't get on the horse ok? It's a lot of work to get off of it."

"Ok look you have been saying a lot of suspect shit! How do you really know my name? How do you know my mother's name? How do you know about the horse?! Jas doesn't know about that!" I balled up my fist, ready to attack.

"Why are you so angry?" Cara asked with annoyance. She walked closer to me and I backed away. She continued, "I told you I won't let anything happen to you and will keep my word. I'm trying to keep you safe. I'm trying to keep you off of the horse. If you would just listen and stop accosting me! I get it; don't trust the white girl! No one wants to trust the white girl, because you never know if she is tryna getcha!"

"Exactly! You don't know this life. You haven't walked my walk. You don't know how many times I have been let down when I trusted anyone in the slightest! And how the hell do you know about the horse?!" I yelled.

Aura burst out of the back door with a fork in her hand and yelled, "What the hell is going on?!'"

"Dammit, Aura I am trying to save her some time. I know what we talked about but I am not going to make her go through that if she doesn't have to. But she doesn't trust me any further than she can throw me and I am trying to walk her through this so she won't end up like the rest of them!" Cara frustratingly explained,

"Ok, all of you are weirding me out. I'm leaving." I said as I turned around and started to march off.

Mai came to the door and stopped me in my tracks. She hugged me like Cara did at the house and rubbed my back. This may seem strange, but I could feel her praying for me. I could feel the warmth and comfort of God as a child would feel being held by their mother. The release of tension and any pain I was feeling as if it was being pulled away from me with silk strings. She released me and palmed my face then said,

"This is a lot for you to process in this moment. Cara is connected to you. We all are. We are not your enemies. It is hard to trust that given what you have been through. But hear me when I say that Cara is eager to make sure you live a fulfilling life. Have you ever been baptized before?"

Before I could answer we heard the bellowing call of Mick entering the house with Reggie.

"Dear Sissy poo! Why ever did you carjack me and galavant your way out to the Hamptons?!"

Mai rolled her eyes and groaned as she turned around and said, "We needed to get away from the chaos that is your house, dearest brother."

Mick smirked and said, "Well this young gent sobered up and was frantically looking for his cinnamon apple spice beloved that you kidnapped."

Reggie chuckled and said, "It's not a problem. I figured she was in good hands if she was with you Mai." He petted my face and kissed my forehead then looked out at Cara and Aura and said, "Good morning, ladies!"

Aura nervously grinned, "Nice to meet you. Reggie right? I'm Aura and this is Cara."

Cara stood wrapped in her shawl with her arms folded and muttered, "Charmed I'm sure."

Reggie nodded and wrapped his arms around me and pulled me into the house. I heard a commotion behind me coming from Cara, but couldn't figure out what it was. Reggie borrowed Mick's car and we headed back to the city.

As I was growing up in the system, one of the most annoying things with people was when they often told me that they understood what I was going through. In my mind, I often wondered how they could understand my pain when they didn't know what it was like living on earth and being separated from their siblings, watching their parents use drugs and being bounced around from one foster home to another because you couldn't and wouldn't allow anyone to control you as if you were an animal. These women were fun, but I hated that they acted like they really knew me or my story.

Over the next two months, we kept in touch though. I spoke to Sis about it and she told me that they had talked about how wonderful I am and that I lived up to the hype. Aura would pray with me a lot and she'd encourage me to see my education journey through. Cara would regale me with tales of her adventures in the city. Mai and I would talk about life, but it always ended with a beautiful word of advice. It was nice to finally have sisters.

Unfortunately, I was facing being let go from John Jay College of Criminal Justice. This was my dream school to attend. Getting accepted into the school gave me hope of becoming the lawyer that I dreamed of. As a child growing up, becoming a criminal lawyer was everything that I dreamed of. I wanted to represent people in the criminal justice system that didn't get a fair trial of the crimes they were committed of. But, my reality was a hard one. After I received word from my counselor that I wasn't going to be able to register for classes until I passed the math exam, I knew that I would have to leave school and focus on whatever I needed to do academically so that I would be able to finish up my degree.

The day I left school I was doing well, but without passing that test there was nothing more I could do. I had started working at a catering hall in Five Towns. Reggie loved me working there because I would bring home free food and my hours were relatively flexible. He didn't like me stressing about school and wondering how I would get back to it.

He would always say, *'Why don't you just drop something? It's easier to live a simple life and I can take care of us.'* To which my reply would always be, *"Doing the bare minimum infuriates me, so no I won't give it up."*. This would always lead to screaming matches between us and I'd usually end up on my back in pleasure or in pain. I kept his aunt's words in the back of my mind that the world was beating him up so he needed me to take the burden so he could be free of pain...it was a purpose; an exalted place.

One day out of determination and defiance I applied at the New York City Department of Juvenile Justice again. When I got the job offer, I called Aura screaming,

"Hermana! I got the job! We prayed on it and I got it! I start in two weeks!"

"Oh my God, that is amazing!! I am so happy for you! We need to celebrate!" Aura exclaimed.

"Yeah! Hold on let me tell Reggie. Baby! Babe! I got the job!" I exclaimed as I burst into the bedroom.

Reggie rolled over in annoyance and mumbled, "What job? You already have a job."

"I applied to the Juvenile Justice job and I got it! I can finally get back to the work I really want to do! There are so many kids who came out of foster care like me that feel like the world is stacked against them, but now I can do so much more for them! Isn't that amazing!" I screeched.

Reggie nodded and said, "Cool," then he rolled over and went back to sleep.

"Um aren't you happy? I won't be at the catering job no more, but this is a huge step! And maybe, I can get back into school and really be able to help them," I said trying to encourage his excitement.

He rolled off of the bed, stomped across the room arriving in my face to the point our noses were touching. Then he grabbed my face, squeezed it, and murmured, "I said, cool. I told you not to be doing so much, but you don't listen! I'm tired, I wanna sleep, and you gonna sleep with me 'til I feel better."

Before I could utter another word he shoved my head into the wall. I whimpered and he became irritated and struck me across my face. I dropped my phone, but Aura could hear everything. I laid on the floor and cried as Reggie stood over me nudging me with his foot insisting I stop crying and that I brought this on myself by not accepting his reply or the fact that he was tired. Aura was crying on the phone and speaking inaudible Spanish. He picked up the phone and hung it up. I eventually cried myself to sleep. Next thing I knew I was in the bed and he was thrusting into me saying *I'm sorry* repeatedly and kissing me all over. I couldn't even enjoy it, I just allowed him to *apologize*.

A few weeks later I was getting breakfast ready before I headed into my new job. I became violently ill and ran to the bathroom. As the bacon burned on the stove I heaved over the toilet. Aunt Sabrina shuffled her way to the bathroom and when I sat up she smirked and said,

"When are you due?"

I ran to the drugstore and got a pregnancy test and took it when I got to work. Sure enough I was expecting my first child with Reggie. When I came home and told him he hoisted me up and spun me around with glee. Finally, we were happy again. Then he said,

"So, I think you should work part time and not worry about school. You can't possibly manage all of that and be a good mother."

I was stunned into silence.

Mick was throwing a fourth of July bash and had invited us all to ride out to the Hamptons for it. Aura called me up and asked me to go shopping with her for the party. We ended up in downtown Brooklyn at the mall, then went for a walk around the city.

"So, you and Reggie; how is that going?" Aura asked

"Okay." I mumbled

"Doesn't sound like it's going okay." Aura stated

I got flustered then explained, "He's going through some things just like everybody else but he's going to be alright, I think. I have a question, why doesn't Cara like him?"

Aura winced and said, "It's not that she doesn't like him; it's the fact that he's a fighter. She doesn't like that quality."

"Well yeah he's a fighter; he's been through a lot. I mean he didn't come through foster care like I did, but his mother didn't love him, his daddy didn't love him, his auntie is the only one that really loves him. So yeah, he's had to fight to be noticed, and fight against people's expectations. That's actually something to really admire," I said defensively.

"That's not what I mean. What I mean is he's always looking for a fight. He's been fighting all his life, and if he's not fighting something or rebelling against something he's not satisfied. He thinks this is normal. He thinks that there's always a struggle, always something to rebel against." Aura stated.

"Well, isn't there especially for black and brown folks?!" I shouted.

Aura sighed and said, "You don't get it to you? All he's doing is playing with his demons and not fighting to defeat them. She just doesn't want that for you. I think that he should be given a chance just like everybody else. But at the same time, hermana, you'll suffer because you are a light in his life and darkness always seeks to snuff out light. Cara's just being protective. You know her life was not a crystal stair at all. Plus, he put his hands on you and frankly that would have been the end for me."

I lowered my eyes and huffed, "So, you don't think I should give him another chance? He is trying to get better. He loves me. He said he would do the work that needs to be done in order for him to feel better; to feel as free as I do. He says I'm worth it. Yeah there are times he is just *being a man*. I know that no one has ever given him a chance. I don't want to be another name on that list. I'm going to fight for him, 'cuz if I don't who will?"

We crossed the street and saw Mick happily trotting along out of the mall with a bag full of clothes. He lowered his sunglasses that matched his black floral top, khaki shorts, and multi-colored sneakers gasped and excitedly said,

"Having a girl's day before we get ready for your clam bake tonight are we?" We giggled and nodded, and he continued, "Most wonderful. Felicia dearest, is your beloved accompanying you for the clams?" Mick asked.

"Yeah, he's coming! He really needs a break." I said excitedly.

"Hey Mick, I need to run home before I head out to the beach house. Can you walk with Felicia?" Aura asked as she looked intently at him.

He lowered his glasses further and questioned, "Right now?"

Aura looked annoyed and snipped "Yes, pendejo! Right now." Aura hugged me and said, "See you tonight, hermana."

As she walked towards the train, Mick and I started walking along the side of the mall chatting about the beautiful Brooklyn skyline. He rambled on about how the city used to be so brown but now everything is steel and glass like the mall we walked past. As we walked, I kept noticing that the reflection in the plate glass windows was starting to change from his vibrant shoes to old church shoes and his shorts to brown pants. I stopped walking and stared at the reflection as Mick rambled,

"There is just no more structural integrity in the city! All we do is throw up condos like weeds and... what?"

I pointed at the glass and he turned his head with the sun shining on his dirty blond hair. He snapped his head back to me revealing the face of an older bald black man shouting, "*Boo!*" I screamed and jumped back while he chuckled and said,

"What's wrong girl?! You don't know your own kin when you see them?"

I squinted and suddenly recognized the man in front of me and whispered, "G-grandpa?"

"DING DING! Call me Pa, girl!" Pa shouted as he smiled and yoked up my body under his arm and we casually walked down the street with his soul shimmering off of the glass onto Mick's body. He rubbed my shoulder said, "Now I need to talk to you for a minute, Felicia, and we don't have a lot of time."

"Um, can anyone else see you?" I asked.

He chuckled in an exuberant tone, "Nope! They see this nickelodeon character walking and talking next to you. But no one cares, it's New York City! Now back to you. Why have you stopped fighting for your life?"

I snapped my head and defensively said, "What are you talking about?! I am working! Things are starting to get better! I'm living with my man and supporting his dreams?"

"His dreams?! That thing has dreams. Of what, being a squirrel? All he does is steal your joy and put you in danger," Pa scoffed.

"He's going through a lot." I said somberly.

"Baby everybody is going through a lot! That's life. He is a grown ass man! He'll figure it out." Pa explained.

I began to defend Reggie, "That's easy for you to say! You had a family! Nobody truly loved him..."

We stopped walking and Pa turned me towards him and cupped my face as he said, "Girl child. Every man and woman have to be a warrior for their own wellbeing. Putting that responsibility on another person is selfish, lazy, and outright abusive." He took his hands from my face and we continued to casually walk against the glass.

"When I met my Etta after the war, I moved her into my little house in a place called Chesapeake City, Virginia. It leaned a little bit, but it was alright. The town was named something different back then. I promised her that we were going to make something of our lives and not be stuck in that shack. Here I was a war hero with a third-grade education promising my baby the world," Pa said as he smiled, remembering.

"Did the Navy give you money after you got back so you could do what you needed to do?" I asked.

"No!" Pa angrily said. He shook his head as he explained, "One day my commander told me and another brother in my regiment to follow this white boy on some mission he had on land. Why the hell were we out with him?! And then we got lost for days! I joined the Navy so I could stay on the boat and not get killed. But anyway, while we were out there, we met another soldier and realized we were children of God that were being used like dogs by the powers that be. They didn't have to take that war home with them, but we did...and I did."

"What do you mean?" I asked

Pa sighed deeply and said, "I got back to Virginia and started sharecropping for a woman named Ruth who had inherited the land. I worked there for about four years before I met my sweet Etta. When we married, I made my promise. Here I was trying to be a Boaz to Etta while working on a field owned by Ruth!"

We both chuckled. Pa leaned up against the glass and part of his spirit started to fade back into the reflection and Mick's head violently shook as if to cast off Pa from his body. Pa's spirit took control of Mick's hand and smacked Mick in the face as he shouted, "Knock it off! I'm not done here!" He straightened himself up and continued,

"I wanted to make good on my promise so in 1952 we left that farm and moved to New York City. We had four little babies, including baby girl Bev. I was 29 years old, living in the big city, working hard, and felt like a king. Etta kept house, I worked, and life was good. But I brought that war home with me and it came out in many ways. My sweet Etta took it all in and sometimes would tell me about myself if we weren't drinking and partying in between. In 1979 my sweet baby died at the age of 49 from cancer. But really, I think it was the grief. I was still fighting the war and she was my soldier because I couldn't be my own. War manifests in the body baby girl and if you don't fight back it'll grab a hold of you and not let go."

"Damn. Are you saying you think you killed my grandmother?"

"Not quite. I am saying I let her fight for me, because I was too scared to continue to fight for myself. I created a space for both of us to be really great, but I couldn't keep up the fight to see it through." He cupped my face once more and said, "You need to be your own warrior baby girl. There is so much to gain on the other side of the battle. You're not a dog, you're a god."

I nodded and suddenly realized that that phrase was very familiar, "Hey wait a second!"

"I've always looked after you baby. Fight back." Pa said as he faded away into the glass and Mick was once again revealed still holding my face.

"Darling...did I blackout? Were we making out?" Mick asked as he looked around confused.

I laughed and shook my head. We kept walking through the city while Mick continued to ramble on about the party and his previous adventures. But the whole time I kept thinking about what Pa said. Being able to persevere is what it was all about. Never giving up was the challenge in the lesson. The glory you want is right on the other side of the war. Sometimes not getting the results you wanted from the beginning will make you feel hopeless, defeated and worthless. Reggie did not know what to do with our baby on the way. How can a man be a parent when all he knows is how to treat a child like an inconvenience? That is his war that he has to fight, but I know that he can't do it alone. So, I guess I will be raising him to be a parent while I raise myself to be a mother. Then we can come together and fight this battle together.

We finally arrived at my door and Mick kissed me on both cheeks and said, "I'll see you all out there. Good vibes only!" ,

"Alright see you later," I chuckled as he marched down the street.

I went upstairs to our bathroom, took off my shirt and looked in the mirror. Staring in the mirror I began to remember when I saw my mother's eyes singing me out of the sunflower field in Tribeland. There was so much hope pouring out of her eyes that I was going to change my life. I placed my hands on my little pouch where our baby was nestled and said,

"Baby, anything worth holding onto is worth fighting for. Don't be so eager to have what someone else has. You have your own place in the world to make an impact. When you get here, we will show you how to put your best foot forward. Mommy is going to do it first. She'll show Daddy how to do it too. This life is now bigger than me and I am not going to give up on myself growing as a woman, friend, leader, or mother. We're going to make it baby."

Reggie had rented a muscle car to drive out to the Hamptons. When he pulled up, he honked the horn incessantly for me to come out. I fumbled with our bag going down the stairs. When I got to the front door I shouted,

"Are you going to come get this heavy-ass bag?!"

"You got two functioning hands. You're a mighty woman, remember?!" He said with a grin.

When I got to the car, he didn't open the door, nor come to help put the bag in the trunk. I threw the bag into the trunk and got into the car in a huff. He teased me halfway out to the Hamptons saying I was being a big baby for wanting to still be treated 'like a lady' but want to have a man's job of having a high position. After a while I tuned him out until we got to the house. Upon arrival to Mai's house, we pulled up front and parked and he hopped out to greet everyone and left me in the car to get the bag.

Cara saw his disrespect and marched towards the car. She insisted on helping me since *my man* did not. I went and sat in our room and cried wondering what the hell was going on with him. More and more people started to file into the house and the party kicked off with the DJ blasting a reggae mix. People gorged on the clam buffet that had an array of seafood and sides and would take off into the party, food in hand, grooving and eating under the summer moon.

Eventually I made my way out to the party and Cara was dancing very well for a white girl. She saw me and grinned, and then came to grab me to dance. I was afraid of shaking too much and hurting the baby, but after a while the beat took over my body and I just let go. Aura and Mai surrounded me, and we continued to dance together as Mick stood up by the DJ's turntables, grabbed the mic and shouted *FREEDOM RINGS!* Suddenly some version of techno and EDM started playing and everyone went crazy.

I saw Reggie from the corner of my eye dancing over by the bar. But then I saw him see me having a great time. He marched over and grabbed me by my arm and dragged me into the house. Cara charged after us but Aura held her back. Mick saw the commotion and began making his way into the house. Meanwhile Reggie began his drunken rant,

"What the hell are you doing?! Out there carrying on like you don't have my baby in your belly!"

"Reggie! I wasn't drinking I was just dancing! I can't have a good time?!" I cried

"Your job is to sit your ass in that room and keep that baby safe!" Reggie screamed.

"What happened to me being a mighty woman that can do anything?" I said snidely.

Reggie geared up to hit me again and Mick marched into the living room and bellowed, "Hey!" Reggie backed up from me and Mick adjusted himself to be more friendly, "Darlings, what is happening here? Aren't we having a good time?"

Reggie became flustered, "She's out there acting a fool leaving me all alone and shit. She knows I'm not feeling well!"

Mick was flabbergasted, "Who pissed in your cappuccino this morning? It seems you're the only one hellbent on having a bad day. Friend...what ails you?"

I tried to smooth over the situation by saying, "He's been having some trouble today. He may just need to lay down. Do you want to lay down baby and maybe we can talk?"

Reggie sneered at me and growled, "There ain't nothing you can do for me except what I asked. If you can't do that I'm out of here."

"Dude, you are confusing the hell out of me. Why would you try and hit the L.I.E. on the fourth of July? Come, let's have a drink and dance, shall we?" Mick said calmly.

Reggie grunted and marched upstairs. Mick wrapped me up into his arms and consoled me as I tried to fight off a sob. He started to hum DMX's *Ruff Ryder's Anthem* and I chuckled,

"Seriously? That's what you're singing right now?"

"DMX is gospel to me darling. I meditate on hip hop hits; it stirs and soothes the soul." Mick explained as he continued to hum.

I felt a gentle touch of an embrace from behind me. It was Mai wrapping herself around me and then she and Mick hummed together and started singing the chorus until I was calm, and we laughed together. Reggie came bumbling back down the stairs with our bag, gave us a side eye, and marched out of the house. I tried to reach for him, but Mick and Mai held me close and encouraged me to stay and try to enjoy myself. I went back to the party, but my mind stayed on Reggie.

The next morning, we took the long drive back to the city and I stared out of the window. My friends laughed and played music completely ignoring my silence. That was alright. I needed to be alone. Coming through the system you learn how to be alone even if you are in a room full of people. Creating that type of solitude so you can ground yourself is a talent. I kept blowing air on the window so I could draw pictures as I wondered why the man I loved was so broken. As we approached the city I took my time drawing a moon with hearts on it and an open flower hanging upside down as I remembered us riding through the city chasing the moon until dawn and he kissed my forehead and plucked a flower from the tree. I stared at the drawing and thought: *Wasn't I enough? He had my love, my attention, my body, and I was carrying his child. What else could he want from me?*

My thoughts were interrupted when Cara looked over at me and threw a car snack at me as she said,

"Hey Gwendolyn Knight, you're awfully quiet over there. You alright?"

"Yeah, I'm ok." I lied.

"Come on sunshine, what's the matter?" Cara asked as she patted my thigh.

"I don't feel well," I said.

"You sick? I told Mick those clams were shaky." Cara laughed. When I didn't return the laughter, she leaned closer to me and said, "Felicia, what's wrong?"

"I'm heartbroken. Reggie is falling apart, and I don't know what to do." I said as I wiped a tear from my face.

Cara and Mai exchanged looks in the rearview mirror and turned and looked back at me worriedly. Mai turned down the music and said,

"What exactly is wrong with him?"

I sighed heavily and started to frustratingly ramble, "He feels defeated. Every time I tell him about how something great is happening, he gets into a slump, says that's great I guess or *cool*, and then gets really irritable. Like my accomplishments are a burden to him. He was like this when I told him about me going back to school, or how I was going to go do work with the foster youth. He only got happy about the baby-"

"BABY?!" They all said in unison.

"Wow. Congratulations. You didn't eat any of the raw oysters, did you?" Mai asked calmly.

Aura nervously smiled and said in a bubbly tone, "Well that's news! I'll get to work on your baby shower."

"You're fucking pregnant?!" Cara exclaimed.

"Glad to know I have your support, Cara" I said while rolling my eyes.

"You're pregnant by that parasite?! How did that happen? Why would you think that this was ok?!" Cara badgered.

"You know what? You are getting on my damn nerves, Cara! You don't know him enough to make that judgement! A parasite?! Really, Cara!" I yelled.

"You just said he can't be happy for you over anything! All he does is bring misery to your life when all you're doing is fighting for your happiness and frankly for his too! He is too lazy to fight for his own life and is sucking the life out of you! Even more so with this child!" Cara shouted.

I glared at Cara and shouted, "Don't you dare bring my child into this!"

"It's her choice Cara. It's her life. If she wants to bring this child into the world so shall it be." Mai stated trying to calm our blistering rage.

Aura turned around in her seat and stated, "The baby will be a blessing and she is going to be a wonderful mother. Give her and this baby a chance. Although I do agree that he is a parasite."

"Are y'all kidding me right now?! He has his troubles, yes, but he is the father of my child and probably going to be my husband. If you can't respect that then we don't need to be friends!" I proclaimed.

They all looked at each other with concern and became silent. We sat in that tense silence until we pulled up to Reggie's aunt's house. I huffed and prepared to get out of the car. Cara grabbed my arm and gently said,

"Felicia, listen to me. You are so special to us. And we don't want anything bad to happen to you or for that matter your child. Reggie doesn't know how to be happy with himself. How is he going to be happy with you and a new life? He can't stand to see you succeed. Do you think he will fight for your life the way you fight for his? He may fight for the child's life out of vanity, especially if the child favors him. Other than that, we-I don't see this going well for you."

I got flustered and said, "You didn't like him from the jump when we met. Do you want me or something? I don't swing your way, boo boo. You're not going to talk me out my draws rubbing all up on me and shit."

Cara rolled her eyes and said, "That was below the belt. But ok...Look he...does...not...love...you. You love him. He benefits from your loyalty to his struggle. You will die with your life in his hands and he will not weep."

Mai sighed and said, "I hate to say it but she's right. We will support you if you decide to keep this baby Felicia. As long as you understand that you are walking into a firestorm of emptiness. You will have us, but you won't have him. He is not built to withstand the pressures of a minimum wage job, and you think he can be a husband and parent? It doesn't work that way. You don't have a baby and suddenly everything clicks."

Aura interjected, "That's not one-hundred percent true. For some it can click, and I think that her hope is that it will." Aura turned around in her seat and looked at me, "Felicia, I know that being without a family makes you want to start your own. But think about your life. Do you honestly think that by carrying motherhood and being a surrogate mother to his insecurities is going to leave room for you to flourish in the way you want to?"

"I can make it work. I have made all situations work before and this is no different. He is going through a transition and that is going to take some time." .

Aura shook her head in disappointment and said, "Transitions don't usually include intentionally causing pain to other people. I knew I should have said something the first time he hit you."

"The first time!" Cara and Mai shouted in unison and were bewildered as they snapped their heads at me. .

I started to sob "You have to give love a chance. No one gave me a chance to be loved. I want to give him a chance to love himself and that takes time. It's took me time and here I am, doing well and thriving more than what anyone said I could. Give him and my baby a chance."

Cara snidely chuckled, "You love yourself and you're allowing him to abuse you? Yeah ok."

"I'm sick of your shit!" I shouted and jumped out of the car with my bag. I slammed the door and Cara opened it back up and followed me towards the steps.

"Felicia! Felicia! Dammit, sis, stop!" Cara shouted

I turned around and yelled, "I'm not your sis! Ever since we met you hated him! I tell you something bad, something that every relationship goes through, and you cast immediate judgement!"

Cara was baffled and laughed, "Immediate judgement! I could look at him and tell he was an asshole! Honestly, I was hoping I was wrong. And here we are seeing you draped in misery and confusion. This is not love! I don't care what he says to you, he doesn't love you. We love you! We speak life into you! We are looking out for your best interests with nothing else to gain. That is real loyalty!"

"You want a damn medal?" I asked

"I want you to be smart about this. The other two may support your decision, but I cannot, and will not support you screwing up your life!"

"Why are you so worried? I'm not a teenager."

"Could've fooled me! In this *Titanic* of a relationship, he's Rose and you're Jack. No room on the door for you! Down ya go all for love that felt good for like what a month?!" Cara shouted.

I smacked Cara across the face and walked away. I heard the other two gasp and Cara huffed and said, "*Ow.*" While I walked up the stairs, I could feel all of them staring at me and didn't care. What did they know? It's not like they all have a relationship and know what real love is. I heard Cara call someone and say, *"You need to get here right now.*" I guessed that I would have to figure out how to squad up with my man because it sounded like she called in a favor.

When I walked into the house, there was a lot of banging coming from our bedroom. His aunt was going to be pissed if he punched another hole in the wall. I marched up the stairs as the knocking and banging got louder. I took a deep breath in anticipation of one of his rageful fits. When I opened the door there was Reggie standing and thrusting into a woman bent over that had box braids and a tattoo of a copperhead snake on her left shoulder.

I couldn't breathe. I couldn't move. I dropped my bag; my mouth was agape. He started saying things to me with an accusatory building rage that went unheard because my heart was beating so loud that it deafened all of my other senses. I never saw the girl's face that he had bent over, because he stood in front of me naked blocking her and sticking his hand in my face fussing and frustratingly rubbing his face. Finally, I heard him say,

"Do you hear me?! You did this! You drove me to this! She has mattered more to me in one day for things she has done to me than you ever will in a lifetime." He paced around, rubbed his face and head as he mocked my care for him, "You-you-you just suck the life out of me and I needed a break, ok? You love up on me and talk to me about my troubles or whatever but then coming to me talking about, *"I got this going on, I got that going on, and I'm having your baby."* What about me?! What about my needs? You can run a whole world and be dropping babies and can't take some time to make love to me the way I want you to? Huh?!" He shook his head violently and picked up his black sweatpants that I bought him and marched up to my face and growled, "You know what though? It's ok. Loyalty. I'm loyal. I'll stay around and deal with that baby. It's a boy, right? I can't do nothing with a girl. We'll work it out. You just need to get your ass in line, stop flirting with my friends and shit and running around trying to be something you ain't never gonna be because you are *my* woman, having my babies, and taking care of this here house I'm building."

I suddenly became bemused and said, "This is your auntie's house!"

He turned away from me then slapped me with all of the might of his back hand. I tumbled down all fifteen of the stairs thumping on every third steps until I hit the floor...on my stomach. I didn't have the strength to cry fully, so I whimpered and sobbed as a knot started to form on my head and blood poured from my mouth. *Reggie no. Why you Reggie?* I held on to my belly and felt it clench and release repeatedly sending shockwaves of pain through my abdomen. Hold on baby. *Hold on. I can still love you through this.*

I crawled towards the bathroom to try and hide from him. He started slowly marching down the stairs, callously laughing at me on the ground. I kept trying to move forward but the pain was searing all over my body; it made it impossible to move my feet or my head. When he made it down the stairs, he turned me over, sat me up against the radiator, clenched his hand around my neck as blood from my mouth dripped on his hand. He spoke just above a murmur,

"Loyalty. This is what loyalty looks like. You take the licks, you take the bullshit, all for the greater good of this kingdom. There are no medals for those held in exalted places, you just do the work." He removed his hand from my neck and wiped the blood on his sweatpants and continued, "No telling if that baby made it or not. With your weak ass genes probably not. Don't worry about it. We'll work on another one. You know I can't make it in this world without you. I'll love you for your loyalty Felicia. Always. As long as you recognize me as your god on earth, I will always bestow favor on you instead of my wrath like today."

The copperhead woman started walking down the stairs and I still couldn't see her face hidden in the shadows. She whispered something to him that I was unable to hear because I became dizzy and was starting to lose consciousness from the pain. Reggie responded and all I could make out by reading his lips was, "*She's ours now.*" The copperhead woman laughed. Then Reggie laughed. And I started slipping away thinking that I once again had nowhere to go and no one to love me.

BAM!

"What was that?!

BAM!

"Was that the door?!"

BAM! Suddenly the door flew open and in rushed Cara, Aura, and Mai. I was relieved as I faded in and out of consciousness. First, I saw Cara wailing on Reggie and cursing him out simultaneously as Aura jumped on his back stabbing him in his shoulders with a fork. Then I saw Mai run up the stairs after the copperhead woman. Next, I saw Reggie screaming in anguish from the stab wounds and Cara laying on the ground with a bloody nose and then getting back up to fight. I heard Mai say, 'Enough! Pick her up and get her out of here.' Finally, I saw Cara pick up his aunt's cane, and with three hard swings, bring Reggie to his knees. After that I blacked out and went into a deep sleep.

When I woke up I was sitting at a table in a shack with sunlight shining through the windows and cracks of the house. There was another powdery stream of light hanging mid-air that was shaped like a loosely bound thick rope, and glowed a white and neon blue color. It hung around the corner into the next room and also out the door. I walked to the window and saw that the rope continued upward towards the distant horizon and I could not see its end. Then I saw many ropes just like it is going in several directions and connected to something in the distance.

Suddenly I heard the shuffle of someone walking up to me. I spun around to see Etta, smiling in her dress and apron, and hand-mixing cake batter. She smiled at me showing off her dimples, and her beige skin with hazel eyes that reflected the glowing rope. Etta put the batter down on the table adjusted her pinned up hair and flung her arms out for a hug.

"Well, you going to just stand there all curious or you going to give your Grandma Etta some sugar?"

I ran over to her and gave her a hug. She kissed my cheek and walked me back to the table to sit.

"You want some tea?" Etta asked.

"Where are we? "I asked.

"My heavenly home. When you make it to this side you can design your own version of heaven." Etta explained.

"I thought all the spirit bodies lived within one body?" I asked.

"Yes and no," Etta said. She gently lifted the light attached to her and said, "You see this? This is what I guess would be a spiritual umbilical cord. We all have our own spaces to just be and are all connected back to our mother spirit Ife. If a descendant of our family needs one or all of us, we all run right through this here cord and we're there quick as a flash!" She laughed.

I laughed, "Were you there, when I came to Tribe land?"

She elegantly chuckled, "I was at the harvest. But no, I wasn't there for the rest of Eva being Eva. Lord, my sister was wild in life so, of course, she is wild on this side too. She always makes her point though."

"Wow this really is a lot to take in. She did say that heaven is a vast space. So, what's this house?" I asked.

Etta smiled and explained, "This is where me and your Pa started out. Although it was brief this was probably the best time of our lives because we had so much passion to seek out a better life. Usually when you want something so bad it starts off small. But then if you nurture it right it'll grow into something you never thought possible. But if you nurture it with anxiety it'll turn into everything you don't want it to be. Much like that squirrel of yours that was beating on you."

A tea cup appeared in her hand and she slowly sipped on her tea and stared at me intently. I lowered my head and said,

"I suppose so. How did I let myself fall so hard so fast?"

"It's not completely your fault. Us Aquarius women have a hard time falling in love with ourselves as deeply as we fall in love with someone else. Shoot, men are like that too. That's how me and your Pa got into the Love Olympics trying, to out-love one another. We lost ourselves in that. It was so wonderful and yet so dangerous because we never grew past the spark. Then it was just survival after he kept hurting from the war you know. Took me out. That cancer and that grief." Etta explained.

"He said the same thing," I said.

"Well, when I saw him on this side, he was on the horse a while because he was aggrieved with how his pain caused my death. I - I told him I forgive him though. You go long enough just surviving, you don't know what living looks like. You can dream it, but unless you do the work you won't get what you want. So, it wasn't his fault...completely. We're good now though." Etta explained.

"So, Aquarius...the Zodiac really is a thing?" I inquired

Etta laughed, "Why yes child. God is organized. Souls are born, popped up to the stars to be organized for their perfect time to be born with the best traits and nurturing of their spirit mothers, then they're born as humans. Everything has its own divine order no matter what you believe. You think it's a coincidence so many people who don't know each other from Adam have similar if not the same characteristics? Ha! Girl we are as unique as snowflakes but we're still all snowflakes. Amen?"

Etta waved her hand and another teacup appeared and filled itself with tea. She insisted I drink up since having someone in your house and not offering them a beverage or food is still rude, even in heaven. I asked about the cake she was baking. We laughed as she said that was just for dramatic effect when we met, since she never got to bake me a cake in real life. The sun's rays continued to twinkle through the house while we walked over to some photos of her and Pa when they were young and in love. Then she showed me the real photos of the people who kidnapped me in the convertible, and they looked like a vibrant modern-day Bonny and Clyde. Next, she showed me a photo of all of her siblings, including Eva, who was one of the most radiant women I had ever seen in my life.

Etta explained how her father, Thomas, married her mother, Clara, who was an Irish woman. Somehow, they pulled off a marriage and had nine children. Unfortunately, Clara died very young and left Thomas to raise all of those children. She sat me back down at the table and said,

"Now baby, why in Sam hell were you all over that man?"

"It was the first time I really felt love. I don't know what that looks like Grandma."

"Well, it's not that!" "Sunshine, when you look in the mirror do you see a dog or a god?"

"I see neither. Without love and or a solid sense of direction, and several failed attempts to making something of myself I see a shell of a woman."

"Lord, child you are dramatic! I can't blame you little water baby. Your worth is not measured in how many people do and do not love you. The only people who you need to worry about are yourself and God. You are a child of God therefore part of you is a God. Like your Pa say, you are not a dog you're a god."

"He also said challenge your god."

"Yes, he did and that means you! Having real love is privilege baby and that starts with you! I know you loved him and understood his pain because it mirrored yours, but it is not a direct reflection of who you actually are. Therefore, you will not love him as you love yourself because he has not paid the price to earn it!"

"But you loved Pa when he was broken!"

"Don't you raise your voice at me! I will take this rope and pop you good!" She sat back down and continued, "Yes, I loved Bobby. More than any man I had ever known. And you know what? As much as I have forgiven him it is still a fact that if I wasn't dealing with all his stuff on top of my illness I would have lived longer."

"Grandma, he is a broken man. I can be a part of his healing. Why can't I wipe the slate clean and just give him another chance?"

The Ife cord started shaking and Etta's face trembled uncontrollably as angry voices were echoing out of the cord. Several faces appeared replacing hers at rapid speed as her head gyrated, and the angry voices increased with inaudible words. Suddenly hundreds of smaller cords poured out of her face and head revealing the faces of all of my female ancestors from Africa, Ireland, and America. Etta's face went back to normal with a tense scowl as the heads circled around me still vigorously rambling amongst themselves until they all said in unison,

"Cause he got you out here looking crazy with a bump on your head!"

Etta and the ancestors rolled their heads and necks as they said, "*Chiiild, girrrl.*" They looked at me with tilted heads, raised eyebrows, and pierced lips. I was in trouble.

I woke up with blurry vision that slowly became clear and saw Cara sitting by my hospital bed. She petted my face and kissed me on the forehead while saying, "Morning sunshine."

As I sat up Cara stepped away and I saw Mai, Aura, and Sis standing in front of me. Sis cried, Mai tried to hide her tear, and Aura had her arms wrapped around both of them trying to keep them calm. They went on to tell me that although Reggie beat me, he will be walking with a limp for the rest of his life after they got through with him. Mick was pacing behind them making calls. It was the angriest I had ever heard him; he spoke with a gravelly tone that was haunting. After he finished his call he ran to my bedside and whimpered,

"Mocha Chips, my darling how are you feeling?"

"Mocha Chips?! Really bro!" Mai exclaimed.

We laughed and while they retold their tales of beating Reggie's ass from different perspectives my mind was racing about everything. I thought about how Reggie became my *why* and he shouldn't have been. Your why is a **constant** reminder for why you are striving to reach your destination. Having faith and believing in what you do is your greatest motivator to keep pushing. This *why* should never make you stray away from your faith in God or yourself, and Reggie did both. Here I was with a support system that offered value to my life. It was going to take some time for me to find my why again. But I learned it wasn't all about winning. Life is about learning to overcome the challenges and not let personal circumstances define you as a person. Paralyzing myself wasn't part of God's plan. The plan was for me to overcome this thing called life.

HOLDING WATER // FELICIA R. WILSON

ROOTED

"Don't go to battle trying to stop a habit. Instead, reshape it
and send it in a new direction."
– Sarah Pullen

I WAS RELEASED from the hospital and Cara brought me to
her and Prism's apartment in Clinton Hill. She explained that
Prism is an Ayurveda healer that works on healing from within
through what you eat, drink, and your soul's alignment. Since
I had nowhere else to go, I went along with it. We walked into
a three-floor walk-up that had certainly seen better days. Cara
carried my bag up the stairs, and we laughed about how they
order out all the time because the steep stairs and groceries did
not mix.

We entered the apartment and walked into a loft style space
with an open kitchen and living room and exposed brick. The
kitchen and living room were painted in a splatter paint of every
color. The round kitchen table was a surprisingly plain mahogany.
There were sitting pillows everywhere, different color drapes
and pictures of goddesses from around the world hung on the
walls or draped in tapestry over doorways. The pungent smell of
cinnamon candles and incense filled the entire apartment that
made you feel like you were somewhere between an orchard and
spice market.

Cara took me to two white sliding barn doors and said,

"This is our healing room. People come here and stay for a few days to be healed through meditation, supplements, and more. Because of all you've been through you'll be here a week."

"I can't stay longer?" I asked.

"Unfortunately, no. We have to keep the space open for others who need long term healing. But we have made other arrangements for you. Although it would mean a lot to me for you to stay longer." Cara explained.

"So... can I stay?" I asked with a hopeful smile

Cara laughed, "No, sunshine. But Aura is already setting up space for you with her and her Mom. You'll be fine."

She opened the doors and revealed a room covered in light blue and white linen hanging from the ceiling that caught the sunlight from the tall window. The was round covered in vibrant pillows and a blue duvet cover and sat in the middle of the room. There was a sitting area by the door that had a small tv tray table so people who are healing could journal. There were different candles that lined the walls and a food table in the back right corner. Cara shuffled my bag inside as she explained that the room was designed to allow the natural medicine to take place.

As I sat on the bed, Cara could see I was confused. She explained that our bodies and souls are connected and both energies are needed to heal ourselves; this is especially true with trauma. While therapy, herbs, prayer and more can be a part of healing we must first dig deep enough to choose to heal so that the rest of the treatments are useful. Once again, I had to drown in my feelings, embrace them, and empower myself.

I laid down and stared at the light dancing through the linen filled ceiling until I drifted off to sleep. After a few hours, I was awakened by the clanking of a tray with a tea kettle and a small plate of brussel sprouts and chicken on my bedside table. Then I looked up to see a smiling middle eastern woman wearing a pink hijab, a t-shirt with a unicorn on it, and jeans with no shoes on.

"Hi, I'm Prism!" she said.

"Prism. Nice to meet you. Cara told me about you. Have to say that's an unusual name." I said.

She casually sat down on the edge of the bed and grinned saying, "For a Muslim girl?"

"No, just period. It sounds scientific. Are your parent's scientists?" I asked.

Prism nodded solemnly and said, "They were." She poured my tea and handed it to me as she smiled and said, "My birth name is Palwasha. It means Light Ray of Moon. But when I was young my parents would always say 'Anything that passes through you for better or worse transforms into a new light. You are our own prism and can change anything.' So, I became a healer. I transform people. That is my purpose." She said it proudly with a smile.

I sipped my tea then asked, "You said they were. Are they retired now?"

Prism folded her lips in, took a deep breath, released them and said, "They were traveling to California on a research grant to test out new energy sources and died in the crash at the Pentagon."

"Oh my God. I am so sorry!" I stuttered nervously, "Did-did you end up in the foster care system?"

Prism nodded and said, "Yes. But who would adopt or take in a Muslim girl after that? So, I begged my social worker to change my name to Prism, to honor my parents. I also figured when potential parents looked at my name they wouldn't dismiss the Muslim girl and think that I was an American girl that just happened to be middle eastern with a unique name. It worked. I got adopted a year later and moved from D.C. to Connecticut."

"You sound American though." I stated

Prism smiled and gleefully said, "I am. But at that time, if anyone looked at me, I was a disgrace. They never took the time to see my light, so I changed myself so they could see it and I could survive. Now, whenever someone dismisses me or makes me feel unworthy, I return the energy with my beautiful colorful light that they can't ignore."

I leaned forward to encourage her and said, "I see your light. You are not unworthy of anything. And you're definitely not a disgrace."

"Right back at you, babes." Prism said as she patted my thigh and popped off the bed. As she walked towards the door she turned around and said, "The tea is nettles and chamomile. It'll make you stronger and help you sleep. All you need to do to reclaim your power is choose to do so. So, drink your tea, rest, and maybe take some time to write these next couple of days.

I laid in that room for a few days and drifted into my overthinking and planning to get myself out of this so I wouldn't have to focus on the pain. It just made things easier. Part of getting myself together revolved around me mapping out a plan and sticking to it. Developing a strategic plan and one that was well thought out became clearer overtime. Creating this plan allowed me to live the lifestyle I dreamed of living. But little did I know, there would be many frustrations and setbacks to deal with as I began to implement my plan for success in this thing called life. However, regardless of the setbacks I kept a great head space and continued to push forward.

The first thing I did was to identify all the things in my life that were unhealthy for my personal and professional development. Any unhealthy patterns I did away with. Next, I changed my surroundings and the people I associated with. Anyone, that took me down memory lane of my past I walked away from. One of the most profound lessons in life I learned was that to change, I needed to do away with those things that brought me darkness and reminded me of my past. In addition, I learned to ask for support where I needed assistance. Whether it was with food, finding employment or even access to different community plans.

On the third day of my healing, I was given some weird tasting herbal tea and did not have an appetite. I was restless. I got up to stretch, then the urge to vomit up everything I had eaten in the last week took over my body. After barely making it to the trash can Prism and Cara burst into my room with two buckets and a towel. I stumbled around the room gasping for air between vomiting. Cara was terrified, but Prism sat down on the bed in a calm manner and calmly said,

"It is well."

I stuttered trying to hold back vomit, "What?! I- I'm throwing up!"

"It is well, you are releasing." She repeated.

I collapsed onto the bed holding onto my stomach and yelped, "It hurts. It's burning my body."

Prism nodded and calmly said, "It is well, your weakness is fighting to stay, fight back."

I started crying as visions or Reggie kept coming to my mind, "Why can't I stop thinking about him? He brought me so much pain."

Prism took a shallow breath and said, "It is well, you placed your value in him, now he is gone. Release his hold on you."

I became frantic and clawed my way around the bed in complete delirium, "Everything is coming back. I went through all those homes. My parents are dead, and I don't know what I am going to do with my life."

Prism pet my head until it stilled my body and whispered, "It is well, a clean slate is what you need. Release the need to hold on to the pain for your strength. It is well. Your body is well. Your spirit is well. Your mind is well. When something knows it is dying out that is when it fights the hardest to stay, especially with matters of the soul. It is well, your medicine is working."

Cara tiptoed over and handed me some mouthwash and encouraged me to rinse my mouth out and spit. Next, she handed me water and I turned over and laid on my stomach trying to catch my breath and calm my body down. I slowly faded back into a slumber as Prism repeated, *"It is well,"* in a melodic whisper as she pet my head.

On day five I wrote about:

When I left Ms. Roberts home in Far Rockaway Queens, and got my first apartment in Rosedale Queens, there were times I struggled to pay my rent. But the good thing was that she would go food shopping and buy groceries for me so that I could eat. She understood that I was struggling but because I talked to her and went to her for support, she showed up. Had I tried to keep my struggles to myself I would have ended up going hungry plenty of days. Mrs. Lee was also a great support system for me. She lived in Laurelton Queens. When I moved from Far Rockaway, she came to get me and all of my belongings. See, Lee was in my life since I was sixteen years old. Her home was my home, and her family were my family. There is, and was absolutely nothing she wouldn't do for me. Once I moved across to the other side of town, she took me to get everything I needed from Ikea. Mrs. Lee was part of what contributed to my overall success because she showed me what having family was all about. Where some people disappointed me, she showed up every single time in my teenage years. She reminded me so much of Ms. Sharon. I didn't have to tell her what I needed; she knew. While Lee helped me get on track with my independence, I kept myself busy. Keeping myself busy helped me focus on staying aligned with what I needed to do to move into success.

I faded out of those wonderful memories and went back to sleep only to be shaken awake by Prism as she calmly said,

"Lovely, it's time to wake up. Your sisters want to speak to you."

She sat me down at the kitchen table with fresh sunflowers sitting in a blue vase. Prism went to prepare some more tea while Cara gently clasped on to my left hand and Aura did the same to my right while Mai and Jasmine smiled at me. They all took a collective sigh of relief and Cara began,

"There will be no more secrets. No more coded speech. No more half-truths."

We all nodded in agreement and Cara said, "Felicia, I'm your cousin."

"My what?" I yelped

"I'm your cousin," Cara laughed, "My name is Cara Levinia Moore."

"Holy shit!" I exclaimed as Cara tightened her grip and lovingly stroked my hand.

Cara sighed and smirked, "Not too long after Aura found me she gave me some tea that put me into a deep sleep where I ended up in the back of a convertible with Illeri and Trey. Or as they introduced themselves to you, Chike and Ife. They took me to Tribeland where I met Aine. You met her remember? Short bubbly Irish woman."

"Oh my God yes! She hugged me and said 'you don't know do you?'" I exclaimed.

"Well, your great-grandmother is my aunt a few generations back. Remember how Pa and Gran talked about Ruth? Ruth's daughter loved and had children with their son. My mother is Black and Irish, but that wasn't acceptable back then so to everyone she knew she was a good ol' Irish Catholic, " Cara explained.

"This is crazy. Now you're telling me I'm Black and Irish? Look at me. I'm a Black woman! I need some proof! You said no more codes and secrets!" I shouted in denial and tried to get up.

Mai quickly placed a forearm length mirror in front of her and it began to rattle. I tried to back up from the table but Cara and Aura held on to my hands and Prism abruptly held my shoulders to keep me in place. I saw my reflection and then a small light twinkled over my face replacing my reflection with the reflection of my Auntie Eva! With a loud echoey voice ringing through the mirror she shouted,

"Girl child!"

"Auntie? Auntie Eva?" I quivered as my transformed reflection spoke my words from her lips.

"No, it's Shirley Chisholm! Yes it's me!" Auntie Eva sarcastically shouted, "Listen here! You two were raised in two different flower fields but are from the same harvest and bloodline. Very rarely does Most High allow us to choose the seedlings to be in our families, but Aine and I chose you and

Cara. You two needed to find each other if it was going to heal the pain of the past so we can move forward. Now cooperate! You have more to learn."

Cara laughed and continued, " I love Auntie Eva. After Aura found me and I went to Tribeland I met Mai and our ancestors came together and told us to find you so that we could start something that should've happened a long time ago.

"Remember the story about the four soldiers," Mai interjected. I nodded yes. "My grandfather was the Japanese soldier. You saw him at the table of jewelry where Madam Colibri popped him. They don't get along very well, but for the sake of our bloodlines they cooperate together. We were there dancing with you in gold the night you arrived."

"Oh my God. Were you just waiting on me to show up all this time?" I asked.

"Not exactly," Jasmine interjected. "My ancestors guided them to me and knew that if I was out of the picture then you would have no choice but to focus on healing. So, they all sought me out and took me to Tribeland. I was *very* skeptical; this is New York, people die for less. But they convinced me when they knew things about my family that only you knew. We weren't counting on you looking up ancestors and when you did Cara responded."

"Sis, you knew!" I exclaimed.

Everyone laughed and each took turns explaining that they coordinated to locate me on the train. Cara stopped me so that

Aura could deliver the necklace to the detention center and deliver the warning about Reggie. Then Mai walked past me and Jasmine to signal her to let me go the day we went shopping. Cara and Mai saw me working at the store and stealing the bracelet, so they reported what they saw which made the manager check the cameras and have me arrested so that I would have no choice but to be in a space of reflection and clarity so that I could enter Tribeland.

Mai and Mick used their money to let me out of prison. Mick got involved by osmosis and would do anything to help his sister. So, he was used to be possessed by my grandfather and create atmospheres to help me get to my healing. Jasmine kept watch and went through her own spiritual cleansing so that she could be a part of the healing process. They tried to keep me away from Reggie, but they were instructed to leave the relationship alone by my Auntie Eva the night we met so that I could learn the lesson of not accepting toxic love that generations of women could not be cleansed from. Cara did not want me to suffer and tried to tell me, but she was stopped. However, when the time came to break me from the pain, she led the charge to beat Reggie so that he would never come near our bloodline again.

Aura tightened her hold onto my hand, took a deep breath and said, "You and I go way back. At least our families do. Many generations ago two Nigerian girls were born in a tribe just a few days apart. Ginika, who is my ancestor and, Omolade, who is yours. While the families had hoped one would be a boy and the other a girl and they could marry they were happy to have them as friends and they were blessed by the □□rúnmìlà priest to always find one another and be a family. Another tribe family,

Lolonyo, was jealous of the blessing because they felt the family was given a special power over the other."

Aura took a big sip of tea and continued to tell me that the girls grew up together until their teenage years. When the captors came a girl from the Lolonyo tribe, that was raised to be jealous, pointed the captors towards the two families' direction in trade of favor. While the captors did take Ginika and Omolade, they also grabbed the Lolonyo girl also. All three ended up on the same South Carolina plantation. While all three suffered for the next three years the Lolonyo girl was jealous of the continued bond between the blessed sisters.

The blessed sisters concocted a plan to serve oleander leaves in the slave master's tea and run away. They weren't sure where they would end up, but they surely did not want to die as slaves. A slave that was renamed Dempsey figured out what was happening and proposed sex to Omolade in exchange for his silence. She refused him and he was completely vexed. The Lolonyo girl spoke to Dempsey as he stomped about the field and he told her what was going on.

The night had come to serve the tea. The Lolonyo girl left the kitchen after the dinner clean up. Ginika went in as she usually did to prepare the tea. She walked into the east wing parlor and served the tea to the master as Omolade waited with two horses outside of the kitchen back door in the west wing. The tea took effect immediately; something they did not expect. Ginika ran through the house screaming for help. The overseer, his wife, and the house doctor came to the parlor to assist the master as she ran towards the back door.

Unexpectedly Dempsey ran up on Omolade and tried to make his offer again and with a hard punch, she refused him. So, he hit both the horses and they took off loudly neighing which drew the overseers to the west wing of the house. The Lolonyo girl stood by the kitchen door and said in Yoruba, *'You won't get far. You don't deserve it any more than the rest of us.'* Ginika ignored her and ran out then saw the horses running away. She and Omolade decided to just run and get as far away as they could. As they sprinted through the tall grass, tangled weeds, and ominous trees, Dempsey pointed the overseers and slave patrollers in their direction.

The blessed sisters ran until they got to the river and found an abandoned boat and oar. When they were about to push off the overseers and slave patrollers grabbed them. Ginika was sold to a man who was trading sugar in the Dominican Republic, and Omolade was sold to another family in South Carolina. Their former master, unfortunately, survived because the Lolonyo girl ran in and saved his life by making him vomit up the poison and giving him water. He bestowed favor over her by making her a house slave and bed wench and made Dempsey the head house slave.

"But the blessing of the Ọrúnmìlà did not waver. Through the generations, a blood relative of Ginika and Omolade has always found one another. Whether as friends, co-workers, lovers, and now us. Getting into shenanigans and always moving forward. Unfortunately, the lines of Lolonyo and Dempsey have always found us; or as you met him in Tribeland, Atawitam. They have been disturbing our peace for generations."

"That's why my Aunt Eva said they're twelve generations of ain't shit!" I shouted.

"Precisely. The man who led the crowd to kill her was a part of Atawitam. And Reggie was no different. Lolonyo introduced your father to your mother and both of them to drugs." Aura explained.

"I was really trying to spare you from any pain. I knew exactly who Reggie was and his soul knew who I was to you. That's why he never liked me and I damn sure didn't like him. Mai reminded me that even if you come from a bad bloodline, you can still change. So, we had to sit back and wait," Cara explained.

"Despite our wishes for you, our ancestors told us that there were lessons you needed to learn on your own. Cara tried to rush past the process." Mai explained.

"I asked them to wait for me to get here before they talked to you about our connection. We've been rockin' since we were in elementary school. While I may not be as rooted as Aura is to you, we are still part of the same sunflower and I love you as deep as Aura's roots go for you." Jasmine said.

"I can't believe that this was all constructed together..."

"For your good," they all said in unison.

"Are you ready to meet more family?" Prism asked.

Suddenly there was a rapid knock at the door. Prism went and opened the door and a very dressed down Mick entered and cheerfully said,

"Oh, pumpkin spice, she looks surprised! I take it you've told her. Don't worry darling it freaked me out too. You probably saw one of my relatives, the dude screaming his ass off to get the harvest party started. " He enthusiastically clapped his hands together and said, "Alright well let's get this possession underway. I have a date at the gym to watch hot men work out."

I started laughing then realized what he said and suddenly became terrified. We all walked to a healing room where a mirror was placed on either side of the bed. Cara sat on the left side of the bed and Mick on the right. Mick started humming *Get Low* by Lil John and the East Side Boys to calm himself down. Aura handed a gold ring to Mick and a emerald necklace to Cara. Mai, Prism, and Aura held hands and I sat on the floor. They began to chant and pray for my ancestors to come.

Ancestors we are calling upon you to use the vessels connected to you now to deliver your message. Connect to your bloodline. The bloodline is the lifeline.

Illeri Trey Illeri Trey Illeri Trey Illeri Trey

Suddenly whispers of their names overtook the room and twinkling lights started attaching to Mick and my cousin. Cara transformed into Illeri in a crop top and jeans, long flowing curly hair and a red lip that accentuated her mocha skin. Mick transformed into a muscular caramel colored man with smooth skin and wavy hair with green eyes. I was frozen in place at what I had just witnessed.

"Hey cuz." Illeri said in an airy echoing whisper. "How you liking your ride so far?"

"Frankly I'm terrified," I said.

Trey chuckled and the laugh shook the room with the bass in his voice, "Don't be afraid. We're family. Well, she's blood, but I am her love so I'm family to you."

"We know what you want and we're here to tell you there's levels to this shit." Illeri said.

"We used to hustle hard, running around in California selling art and jewelry in the late 70s. First it was legit, then we got desperate. So, we did everything we could to survive until we became more successful." Trey explained.

"The phrase to get what you've never had you must do what you've never done is dangerous. It is pleading for you to do something illegal to get you there faster. We sold drugs, got caught and killed." Illeri said.

"For you, you chase success like you chase a bad man, cuz. Making erratic moves when your soul ain't right. Your heart and soul gotta be in the game to level up your purpose not your profit." Trey said.

"You want to save kids like you right? That's cool but if you are approaching it for the glory and not the purpose you will end up beaten and empty like the way Reggie has left you." Illeri said.

"What am I supposed to do?" I asked.

"Chase success like you chase a relationship with God. God does not ask much of us if you think about it. It is simple. Carry out your purpose and have a good time. We had a great time, but we lost the vision." Illeri said.

"You need to continue to get to know your roots so you will know how to plant and nurture your spiritual garden. Essentially, get your soul n' shit straight like Jazzy say." Trey chuckled.

"Clear the bad roots, cuz, and make room for new growth. It is truly your choice to plant the same bad seeds and hope for better or to start anew." Illeri said.

I became frustrated, "But...HOW?!"

They smiled at me and said, "Jump in."

The light of their souls withered away and went back into the mirrors and Mick and Cara collapsed on the bed. My sisters surrounded me, and I began to cry uncontrollably because now I was more confused than ever. I wandered back to my room and laid there while Mick and my sisters rested. Per usual, I was anxious and started planning once more.

I needed to focus on my life story. I began writing down what I went through and began developing a healthy mind by telling myself I am better than my struggles than that into which I was born. To add, I began tracking my progress of what I wanted in life compared to my present position. I reiterated to myself what my long term and short term goals were and what I needed to do stay focused.

By implementing this system, it allowed me to catch any slip ups and make the correction to get back on the road to success and accountability. While holding myself accountable for my own downfalls, I envisioned where I wanted to be and started taking those steps to make it a reality. As I began weighing my career options, I constantly told myself that I wanted to transition from working for a company to owning my own.

I started to envision what it would be like to speak on adoption and foster care platforms. I began to reward myself. Then I thought about rewarding myself as a habit. Maybe going to the spa and personal movie time just to name a few. Finally, I learned to be patient. As a kid I always wanted things to happen when I wanted it. Little did I know that everything in life didn't work that way. I had to learn fast that. As I began to grow as a woman, sister, friend and mate, it was then that I realized for me to grow in different aspects of my life, I had to go through challenges, disagreements and some setbacks. What I learned in these moments were that life was preparing me for the improvements I needed to help me develop. Going through foster care helped me to understand that I was a work in progress and in order to get to the other side I would have to do the work and make all the changes necessary to break the chains that were holding me captive. Immediately, I began to shift lanes and focus on progress and not perfection. I began working on me inside out. Part of working on me meant that I needed to first address my childhood trauma. To develop healthy habits, I needed to re-adjust and improve my overall quality of life on a continuous basis. That meant I would need to work on me, day in and day out. Honestly, I found it to be a scary process because the outcome was unpredictable. However, not knowing the outcome was thrilling. I knew doing the work would mean that I had to challenge myself to go places, both good and bad.

Every day I woke up I started my day off by saying something positive and releasing it into the atmosphere. This includes prayer or a simple affirmation. Throughout the day, I would reflect on that prayer or affirmation to keep me in a safe and peaceful place. This included my mental, physical, spiritual and emotional wellbeing. The more progress I continued to make in life the more I was able to help others. Creating and implementing daily habits helped reassure me that I was on the path aligned with what I was supposed to be doing to show up in the world. (You started this paragraph in one tense and then went to past tense. Changes reflect past tense to show what you did to put you on your path.)

HOLDING WATER // FELICIA R. WILSON

CROSS THE RIVER

〜〜〜．〜〜〜

"Don't forget to pause and nourish yourself a bit along the way. When you're born to help others sometimes you forget to help yourself."

– Paula Heller Garland

AFTER FINISHING MY week at Cara and Prism's, I moved in with Aura and her Mom, Christina. She taught Aura the way to get to and from the spirit world and function within any faith someone followed with the basic universal principal of love. Christina was very loved by a man named Fernando. When they met, he was being attacked by a mugger and she ran up on him and stabbed the attacker with a fork. As it turned out this was a family trait that went back generations because they found it to be more efficient. They fell madly in love, eloped, and had Aura. But unfortunately, he was killed in a car accident and Christina never loved again. Determined to be connected with him she started praying to see him and he showed up in her dreams and explained the spiritual world; knowledge that was now passed to Aura and the rest of us.

Mama Christina was feisty, but kind and loved her dog Didi, a yorkie with a very opinionated bark. She welcomed me in with open arms. We talked about my experience so far. She could tell that I was still feeling disconnected although I had so much information in front of me. Mostly, I had a hard time looking in the mirror because I had subjected myself to so much pain;

I hated that part of my story. One morning while Aura walked Didi, Mama Christina asked me,

"So, what's your full story, mija?"

"Mama, I don't have much of a story outside of what Aura told you," I said.

"Mierda, girl! Every soul got a story. Usually, it starts when they discover their soul's purpose or perhaps on their way to. Maybe even learning how to love the season or skin they're in."

"I'm still trying to love the skin I'm in. I just see my parents' pain most of the time." I said solemnly.

Mama Christina sighed and said, "The way we look is a result of either love or trauma, but we here walking in it. It is the book cover to an incredible story. Don't shame the grace of God by being a boring read. Get into some adventure. So, what's your real story?"

I went on to tell her how we all came together, and she was so happy that we all connected the way we did and that my healing was underway. I told her I was still hurting from Reggie, although some of the toxicity had worked its way out of my system. She smiled and said,

"God gave power to a lot of things but there is something about love that is unmatched. People crying and carrying on when things they think are love don't go their way. But part of love is wisdom. And you aren't going to get wise sniffing roses; you got to let the thorns stab you a tad so learn how to hold it properly."

I got flustered, "Why do the spiritually wise always speak in metaphors?"

Mama Christina laughed, "To give you the power to think and change. If we outright told you the right way to go your hardheaded ass wouldn't listen! But if you have to take the time to decipher the riddle in the metaphor then you appreciate the answer more when you finally figure it out."

I decided to go back to church to get re-centered. While I'd quite literally seen the other side, I needed to feel some sense of normalcy again. When I would go to church before it felt like I belonged to something. A community, a family of believers that were possibly just as broken as I am. Although my body was healing and I had been doing the soul work with Aura and Mai, my heart was still broken, and my head was still all over the place.

I took a cab from Harlem to my church in Queens. Trying to get my head right and my head was everywhere. My head drifted off into the clouds as we zipped through the cars then hit traffic, zipped some more and then hit more traffic. The cab driver was cursing out the cars like that was going to make them go faster.

As I began to incorporate the different levels to putting my life back in order, life became more clear with the path that on which GOD placed me. . I remember the day that I stepped into the now. Doing so, I've been able to lift the baggage of my past while gently and slowly walk into my calling. But, for me to be able to fully release all the weight holding me down, I had to find ways to keep myself in good spirits.

As a kid, it was difficult for me to adapt to things and live a normal life like most of my peers. I didn't have the luxury of a household filled with constant love, nurture, and ongoing support. . When I was first diagnosed with depression, I didn't understand it. As time went on, I would feel myself being sad, withdrawn, and often lonely. When I began taking the medication daily, it would help suppress all the feelings and ups and downs I was going through.

As time went by, my body became more numb to the troubles I endured from my childhood. Being depressed made me feel anger towards everyone. It didn't matter if it was myself, foster parents, social workers or the psychiatrist treating me. As I began to sink in my own misery over the years, it became clear that the only way I would be able to beat my depression was to find a way to cope, find a way to alter my way of thinking and put it into motion.

We pulled up to the church and the taxi screen said my order was $4.22. I was shocked and thought that this had to be a glitch. I called it to the cab driver's attention. He looked on his meter and started flailing his arms around having a fit! He started bashing his meter and cursing it out in a blended gibberish of English and whatever language he spoke. Finally, he said,

"It's Sunday. Just go. I'll get blessed another way."

I tried to hand him money and he refused it and waved it off, so I hopped out the car before he changed his mind. As I was walking up to the church there was a white man in shades walking up the steps in a fuchsia colored suit. When I looked closer, I realized that it was Mick! I ran after him and shouted,

"Mick! Mick!"

"Darling. My sweet, what are you doing here in Queens?" Mick whispered as we entered the church, and he removed his glasses.

"What are you doing in Queens at a Black church in an Easter suit in September?" I chuckled.

"Beloved Buttercup, I am always in style or at least a feature attraction," Mick shamelessly answered as he strutted down the aisle to a seat.

I followed him and scooted into the pew where he was. The seats were numbered in the church, which I always found odd. My seat number was 22 and his was 21. The organist began to play some music as Mick was flipping through the program. I nudged him and said,

"Hey, why do you think they number the seats?"

"I don't know Truffle. Maybe if they call your seat number you get a prize," Mick stated sarcastically as he continued to flip through the program.

He stopped on the reading of the day which was Deuteronomy 4:22. He pulled a travel size Bible and a magnifying glass out of his jacket pocket and opened it to read the scripture with his visual aid. I started chuckling and asked,

"Mick why are you using that tiny Bible? There are some here that you don't have to squint at."

"I've had this since I was a child. It's special. Now hush; I'm reading," Mick snapped then winked at me.

"So, what does it say?" I asked.

For the first time I saw Mick have a very stoic face and said, *"I will die in this land; I will not cross the Jordan; but you are about to cross over and take possession of that good land."* He put down his mini Bible and magnifying glass and said, "Well darling that's awfully depressing. To come so far and not be able to cross into the promised land because your past is holding you back."

I chuckled and said, "I think it's a little deeper than that."

"Not for me sunshine, not for me." Mick got teary eyes and stared forward waiting for the service to start.

"Mick what's wrong?"

"If we want something different, we have to do things differently. But sometimes it's just hard to let go of what you know when you're comfortable with it. And it holds you back from what you really want because you're terrified of living without that chip on your shoulder. I have 100 chips to get rid of, but I can't because they make me magical. And I'll never cross that river because I can't live without my magic. It might be a purposeless existence, but it fills me up." Mick explained solemnly as he picked up the church fan and started fanning himself.

I asked, "Do you-do you still talk to Reggie? He was empty like that too."

He gasped and covered his mouth with the fan and said, "Oh, Honeydew Melon, he is not my portion." He continued to fan himself and said, "I do not associate with abusers. You can abuse alcohol, drugs, or someone else's money and that is totally forgivable in my book. But beating up on people? *Tssk...* no ma'am. When Mai told me what happened I blocked him on the phone, social media, whatever you can block people on and reported him to the authorities."

"Did they pick him up?"

"Yes, to my knowledge, but I have lost track since then." He stopped fanning himself, put his arm around me and said, "We may both feel that emptiness, however I fill my emptiness with uplifting people. He fills his emptiness by bringing others down into his pain so that he does not have to deal with it. And that's not healthy."

"Neither is throwing parties every chance you get to cover up your pain," I said.

Mick looked at me, lowered his eyes and said, "Then how would I have friends?"

"I'm your friend. One is better than nothing."

"Oh, Plumpy Plum. Yes, yes you are my friend. You want to know why I started throwing those gregarious outlandish parties? Well, when I was eight years old my parents gave me up for adoption. They were wealthy and I had become an inconvenient truth. I was, what is known now as pansexual, and they could not accept that. It was bad for their image. So, they medicated me to no end thinking I would change. And by the 10th or 12th medication they realized that it wasn't working, and the medicine had left me with an empty shell."

"Oh my God."

"Yup. I got adopted after a year at the agency. Then when my real parents walked in with Mai, she chose me and wrapped me up in her love like a big sister even though I'm two years older. She was the only person to accept me for who I am on the surface and the emptiness underneath. So, our parents kept me, did not medicate me, but the pain ran deep. No matter what they did to make me happy, it just didn't work. I didn't like that feeling of being an emotional burden. So, I threw a big party on my 18th birthday and realized I could turn my emptiness into a tool for healing others. Anything can be repurposed, Sugar Plumb."

"Have you ever met Prism, Cara's girlfriend? She has really helped me."

"I have...the thing is I am not ready to be whole yet and face the truth. I'm just not strong enough...not yet. Be that as it may, I know what you all have been up to and I think it is awfully courageous for you to tap into your inner goddess. Things are going to get rough and I am here to help in any way I can. Even if it is to a ghost's puppet so you can get your messages."

We laughed and I said, "You think you'll ever seek wholeness?"

"Not anytime soon darling. I am in love with the magic of putting on the show."

I laid my head on his chest and reflected on the day my foster mother gave me my medication and I pushed it to the back of my mouth hiding it under my tongue. When I left her room, I ran to the bathroom and spit it out. That day was the beginning of redefining me without using medication to cope and move on. To move forward, I had to find solutions to replace the feeling medication gave me. First, I learned to give myself time and have a daily one on one conversation with God before I really knew how to talk to the Most High. Because I grew up in the church under the Baptist faith, I was taught from a young age that keeping God first was the way out of hurt from the world. Ms. Sharon would often say, "cast your worries unto GOD and allow him to guide your path". I challenged the God outside of me, but really it was the God inside of me that I needed to acknowledge.

Pastor preached a word that seemed to circle around the point of the message. I hated those types of sermons that seemed like they were playing Scrabble with scripture hoping it's a word with which we would agree. It was not until he paused for a moment and held his chest that everyone sat up in their seats thinking he was having a heart attack. Mick sat up further and nudged me to point at the light that was coming from the window.

"Pumpkin spice latte! Cherub, the Pastor is being possessed!" Mick loudly whispered to me.

"Are you sure?" I asked.

Mick gave me an exaggerated side eye, "Don't you think I know?!"

Pastor readjusted himself, raised his hand to calm the worrying crowd and continued, "Deuteronomy 4:22...that's something special there. Let's look at that again. Moses could not cross into that good land because he had completed his tasks and those he led were to prosper from his completed mission. How many of us are allowing our past pains and journeys to revoke access to the heaven within? Let me clarify. Did someone rob you of love? Were you abused in any way? Did the generations before, maybe 12 deep, create a curse over your life that you are holding on to because it's all you know? The numbers 4 and 22 tell us you need to have faith in yourself and create the heaven within so your spiritual prosperity can begin in you. Let the harms of the past retire their space in your life and seek refuge within where God resides and is waiting for you to let him in and prosper your soul. Clean up that mess that won't let you see the heaven within and God's love around you."

Mick and I nudged each other insisting that his message was for one of us. After service Mick and I walked out in linked arms and stopped to see Pastor. He shook Mick's hand, then took mine and whispered loud enough for Mick to hear, "Your Uncle Charles says hello. Thank him for me for cleaning up my sermon." Our eyes bugged out and we nodded then scurried out the door!

After I calmed down, I decided to dig deeper and take my Uncle's advice. I would read a lot. Often, when my mind was all over the place I could not think straight. Reading became part of the stability for me to adjust the busyness of my mind. One of my favorite books was the "*Lost Boy*" and "*A Child Called It*" by Dave Pelzer.

Dave Pelzer was relatable. While going through my own personal battles, he gave me hope. Like myself, he was abused but by his biological mother. Dave later found refuge when he was rescued and placed into a foster home. Looking at Mr. Pelzer's story helped me realize that taking the pain of what you've been through, and turning it into purpose and power to change the world, meant that you were now in control of your own story. Like Mr. Pelzer, I had decided to re-write my own story, but I needed more ink first.

It had been a month since I left Reggie. I was doing all I could to reconnect to heaven within as my Uncle Charles said to do. I continued to do my meditations, prayers, and finally finished my ancestor alter, although I think Mama Diana got irritated about running into it by the kitchen every day. Jasmine had come back for another visit to check on me, but also to enjoy tea and walking in Central Park in the fall with me like we always did. It was our way of being bougie before we knew better but we still enjoyed it. As we walked there was an African man drumming and a woman singing their own version of *No More Drama*, by Mary J. Blige, one of my favorite songs that got us both through so much grief. Her outlook on life and love reminded me that even through the hurt and pain I needed to push through to get to the other side. Jas started dancing to the music. She encouraged me to dance,

"Girl, you done got rid of that rat! You better come on and dance."

Before I could decide to dance, she pulled me in front of the mini park band and they erupted in a harder beat and melody.

The woman did her version of Mary's famous growl during that song and sang 'No more drama" over and over as the man played to our energy dancing and spinning around. We finally tired out and the duo nodded to us and said, "*Asè.*"

Later that afternoon we got together at a cafe in Manhattan talking about work, life, and knocking a few back. Cara jumped up from the table and scrambled to the bathroom as the several drinks had hit her bladder. We all laughed, and Prism looked up and saw a familiar woman across the room dressed in an orange and green maxi dress with black jewelry. I couldn't see her face, but she slithered through the crowd towards us.

"Oh no." Prism gasped.

"Oh, hell no!" Aura aggressively added as she grabbed the nearest fork.

"Ladies, stay calm." Mai ordered

"Who is that?" I asked.

"Lolonyo," they all said.

"If we don't engage her then maybe she'll just go away," Mai said.

We all turned away from her, although I still couldn't see her face as she moved towards us. Suddenly we heard a loud *thwack*! It was Cara slapping the Lolonyo girl clear across the room. The crowd on the dance floor backed up, gasping and whispering, "*Oooo girl, what she do? Is she alive?*" Cara kept gunning for her, and Prism and Aura had to hold her back as the Lolonyo woman tried to sit up from the floor.

"Don't even think about it, bitch! I'm sick of your shit! You want her, you're gonna have to get through me!" Cara boldly proclaimed.

Prism and Aura pulled Cara away while Mai and Jas hustled me out the door. My sunflower sisters followed behind us still trying to calm Cara down. My cousin kept pacing and trying to breathe. Prism frantically searched her purse to find a blunt. She finally found one and handed it to Cara who was nearly hyperventilating. She was shaking so much that she could not light it and snatched it out her mouth and shouted,

"She has come so far! I can't let that "ain't shit" bitch disrupt her peace!"

Mai took a deep breath put her arms around Cara and said, "If we're going to protect her, we need to equip her to handle anything that is coming her way. She knows your heart is full of love and truth, but Cara, this is not your fight it is hers." Mai turned to Aura and said, "Aura, let's take a ride, it's time."

We walked back to Mai and Aura's cars in an uncomfortable silence as Cara lit her blunt and Prism rubbed her shoulders, whispering, "*It is well.*" I hopped into the back of Aura's jeep with Jas, and Cara sat in the front, put on her seat belt and reached back to rub my hand to reassure me that she was ok. Prism and Mai pulled off ahead of us and we sped off behind them. As we traveled through the city towards the highway with the wind whipping through the topless truck I yelled,

"Where are we going?"

"All this time, and you're not use to us kidnapping you?" Aura yelled back.

We all laughed and continued on our travels. I fell asleep as the sun was setting on the Long Island Expressway. At this point, I figured we were heading out to Mai's beach house. No telling what we were going to do this time, although I had hoped there'd be snacks since I didn't get to finish my food at the lounge. I could feel that we had gotten off the highway and were turning on more residential roads. Jasmine shook me awake and I saw we were passing a sign that said Mattituck. I sat up and Cara was kneeling in her seat staring at me, smoking.... again, and smiling.

"Well, you're feeling better." I chuckled.

Cara smiled as smoke escaped her mouth, "Yeah I am. You want a hit?"

"No, I'm good," I said

"Didn't Ileri tell you that this was faith, cousin?" Cara asked.

"Yes, but faith don't get you high though," I said as I chuckled. and chuckled

Cara grinned and said, "It will if you're practicing it right. The same way you can get your praise on in church and feel the power of God in you is the same feeling you get when you're high. Like you can do anything. Like you're connected to everything and everything has its own energy around you. But it doesn't scare you, it overtakes you, and you never want to be without that balanced feeling of phenomenal cosmic power and the vulnerability of flesh. You gotta take it in doses because it can drive ya a little bit crazy. So, we share it amongst each other, come to revelations together, share the power together because none of us can wield it all on our own. The world or the full comprehension of God. So cuz, wanna take a hit?"

She offered the blunt to me again and I took a puff. The smoke filled my lungs but then as I released it, I felt an ease on my body, like I breathed out my worries. Cara took it back, then winked at me and said,

"Atta girl."

We pulled up to a field of sunflowers and Jasmine and Aura hopped out the truck. Aura ran back and rustled through her collection of forks and grabbed a switchblade. Jasmine held different sunflower heads still as Aura sliced off six of them. They returned to the car and Jasmine took my hand and explained.

"We're going to baptize you today."

"I've been baptized before girl! I don't need it again!"

Everyone laughed and Aura sighed and said, "You may have been baptized before, but since then so much has attacked your spirit. It's time to wash it away with the help of our ancestors."

As we pulled up to the oceanside and walked down onto the beach she continued to explain that they were going to call on all of their ancestors to rid the infestation that had taken root in me by generational curses. Cleansing can be done repeatedly;

however, it was important to get rid of the spiritual filth that was circulating in my soul. I was initially confused because I thought the cleansing I did with Prism got rid of all of that. Aura continued to explain that the mind, body, and spirit are separate entities that also work together, and I had cleared my body and mind, but my spirit was still attracting curses.

The sunflowers they cut were to connect our physical selves with the spiritual realm along with ancestral jewelry that would signal the spiritual bodies to join us. Mai and Prism stood at the ocean surrounded by white candles. Prism held some blessing oil in a glass jar that once belonged to her mother. Mai smiled at me and said,

"Do not be afraid, we are in this with you. You are not pure, but you are not unclean and deserve a new start. This is going to be intense, but your body is finally strong enough to handle it."

"Wait!" I exclaimed, "I don't have any ancestral jewelry to call upon Ife."

"I do." Cara smirked and winked.

Jasmine handed out the sunflowers one by one and Aura handed out the jewelry. Each sister attached the jewelry to their sunflowers. Mai had an emerald ring that was left by her mother. Jasmine had a pearl bracelet that was her grandmother's. Prism had some gold bangles that were left by her mother. Aura and Cara had matching wood carved necklaces that two descendants of our original ancestors owned. Prism anointed each of the flowers and jewelry and handed me the last sunflower. Then she anointed my head, my sisters surrounded me and walked me into the surf. They pointed their flowers at me, and Prism sang,

"Aghslini!"

Followed by Mai, "Arainagashite."

Then Aura, "Lavarme."

And Jasmine, "Wash me away."

Then finally Cara, "Fọ mi kuro."

A giant technicolor wave came hurdling towards us and we fell backwards into the wave together. I was dragged deep into the water until I fell into a tube-like structure and landed face down and was suddenly dry. I turned over and saw a faint light above me and dark shadows swirling around me. Panic took over when I realized that I was in the well. Suddenly I heard hard banging from above and a deep hum of voices. Water began to form below me and start to push me from the top as the dark shadows swirled around me and slowly formed into horse heads with glowing red eyes, snarling at me as I continued to rise.

When I reached the top, the horses swarmed around me blocking my view from what was causing the booming sounds and hum of voices. They kept talking to me saying things like *dependency, weakness, laziness, unlovable, emptiness, dishonesty, faithless, cursed blood, you are of cursed blood.* With every word they spoke it was harder to breathe. I held my chest and tried to balance on top of the swirling water beneath me and suddenly I heard a loud voice break through the neighs and growls of the horses that swarmed me,

"Get away! I said get off of her! Wẹ Wẹ Mọ! Wẹ Wẹ Mọ! Wẹ Wẹ Mọ!" The strong voice said.

The horses began running in and out of my body and continued to swarm me but created enough of a space for me to see the strong voice calling out was Beverly! She ran around me with a bundle of burning sage as she screamed for the horses to remove themselves from me. The more she advocated for my soul the more the horses disappeared and revealed my sunflower sisters screaming the same for me as they performed a dance that had them scuffing the ground with their heels, jumping in the air, and thrusting their arms forward as if to pick up and throw away pieces of the demons that surrounded me.

Then I heard a roar of voices chanting as each horse kept running through and around me and exploding into dust, "Wẹ Wẹ Mọ Wẹ Wẹ Mọ Wẹ Wẹ Mọ. Cleanse. Cleanse. Cleanse."

With each horse dissipating it revealed all of the tribes connected to my sunflower sisters strung together by their soul cords chanting for these demons to leave me alone. They beat the ground with their feet, raised their voices, shouted in their respective tongues and then my tribe's original language repeatedly as each horse became weak, or exploded and disintegrated. The loudest voice that encouraged the crowd and chased the horses away from me was Beverly.

I saw the same fear in my mother's eyes as they were in the well, yet something came over her to push past the fear of the horse she recognized, cursed blood. The horse grew larger and sprinted around me saying in a booming echoing voice, "*Cursed blood cursed blood.*" Beverly kept running after the horse as she whimpered and cried out in a loud rageful voice,

"A fi ẹmi rẹ fun Ọlọrun! A fi ẹmi rẹ fun Ọlọrun! Your life is given to God, Felicia! I offer up my baby for God's power and grace! Get away from my baby demon! You took me; you will _not_ take her! Get away!"

The horse responded, "And what makes her so special to defend? She is a cursed woman, born of many cursed women. This only ends one way."

Jasmine stood firm and shouted as a spirit cord wrapped around her, "She is my sister!"

Aura yelled the same as she got connected to her spirits. Then Prism bellowed the same and Mai screeched the same. Finally, Cara proclaimed,

"She is my sister!"

"She is my blood! And you will not have her!" Beverly and Cara yelled in unison.

Cara stretched out her arms as her spirit cord pierced through her back and attached itself to Beverly and they both screamed, "Yekikikikikow!"

The rest of the tribes' cords lit up, and my sisters repeatedly yelled "Yekikikikikow!"

The horse began to shrink in size and slowly diminish as the cords and praising warrior voices of Chike and Ife and all my sisters lit up the sky and destroyed the horse of cursed blood. It burst into flames and the debris fluttered away.

The water beneath my feet loosened and I dropped back through the well and arrived back in the ocean with the sun gently kissing the horizon. I laid their floating for a moment as one by one my sisters rose up from the water. We all floated in the ocean for a moment catching our breath. Then Cara broke the silence,

"Woo! We did it!" She screamed and flipped over in the water and swam to hug me.

The rest of my sisters smiled and smothered me in hugs and joyful giggles. Our embrace was broken when Aura felt something swim past her leg and panicked. She yelped and attempted to high knee her way out of the water. We cackled and started to slowly make leave the water.

We made our way back to Mai's beach house and spent the night laughing and drinking our way into a deep slumber. When I woke up, there was Cara sitting outside looking out at the water in her shawl, although she wasn't smoking this time. I made my way outside and down the pier as the sun began to peak over the horizon. She smirked at me and opened up her shawl to invite me in as her bare feet dangled over the edge of the pier.

"Your feet aren't cold?" I asked

"Nah. I like the feeling of the cool morning air on my feet," she said casually.

"Well, the cool morning air isn't doing your breath any favors," I laughed.

"Right back at ya! What is that; Apple Crown Royal?" She laughed. "Remember last time we spoke out here and I told you I was talking to God?"

"Yeah. I just thought you were high though," I said.

"Fair point," she laughed. "If you look out on the horizon you'll see what I'm talking about. It's the eyes of God.

I sat there with my cousin watching the sun cascade and spread out over the waves. Then there were some shadows of people in the distance. As the sun took over the sky the shadows seemed to disappear more. While I knew what was happening scientifically, I knew what the other side looked like and figured out that the people we call angels come to us in the night and in the day. The souls connected to us were the eyes of God, watching us always.

It was time to assert agency over my life and take care of myself in mind, body, and soul. It didn't mean I wouldn't need help to cleanse or to seek the heaven within for guidance. Now that the wild horses carrying the burdens of the past had run out of me there was space to plant healthy seeds and allow them to grow.

Cross that river into the promised land, there is nothing holding you back.

HOLDING WATER // FELICIA R. WILSON

BROKEN MIRROR

"The most important thing any broken individual can do is
keep their chin up and keep moving forward."
– Matt Hardy

WHEN YOU MAKE the decision to assert agency over your life,
you create the opportunity to be greater than you ever imagined.
I saw how this unfolded over the next two years with myself and
my sunflower family. We all needed a sense of direction that was
beyond our spiritual healing and took the chance to manifest
beyond ourselves.

I went back to school at John Jay College and was studying
Criminal Justice so that I could work with troubled youth that
were in and out of foster care. Jasmine had come back from
upstate New York and was working as an executive assistant to
an Executive Director at a child welfare agency; she gave me a
lot of insight on how the other side worked. Aura moved out
of her Mom's house to start her own healing center after being
under the tutelage of Prism and Cara. I stayed with Mama so I
could save some money and continue my spiritual practices.

Mai used the rest of her inheritance money to create a
foundation that urban community organizations could benefit
from. Prism decided to go to medical school and grow her
knowledge in western and natural medicine. Cara got her
certification to be a counselor for youth and stopped smoking
as much weed; she still needed some after dealing with the kids.

Mick opened a bar in midtown Manhattan and a rehabilitation center right across from each other; he said he did it that way because, *"People have the right to choose how they want to process their shit."*

Then, after the first Black President, Barack Obama, was elected in November of 2008, Cara and Prism decided to get married that following spring. Because their marriage was not legal in the United States, but it was in Canada, they decided to get married in Niagara Falls on a boat that was licensed in Canada so their marriage would be legal. Mick drove us up to the wedding. It was one of the most beautiful sights I had ever seen.

Cara and Prism had the boat decorated in all white with lace, jewels, and table cloths and cutlery, with the exception of bright sunflowers on every table. Prism's dress was a traditional Muslim cut style that completely covered her, but when she walked, the jewels on the dress shimmered, making her walk in rays of color. Cara's dress was a sapphire blue ball gown with a sweetheart neckline and pleated chiffon in orange, pink, and purple. When they stood together they looked like the birth of the souls in Tribeland, and the sunrises that Cara loved so much.

As we sailed through Niagara Falls, Mick ruled the dance floor in his purple suit and white fedora demanding everyone join him and the brides to dance. My sunflower sisters and I sat and laughed together.

"So, when you are you going to go on a date?" Jasmine asked.

"Sometime between next week and never." I replied and she snickered.

"Girl! Life is short. It is s-h-o-r-t. If you don't take the chance to give love a chance, you will regret it the rest of your life." Mai explained.

"Well, last time I fell in love we had to nearly do an exorcism!" I exclaimed.

"Ase." They all laughed.

"Hermana...sometimes we hold on to things that we feel like will never happen again. That is for better or worse. Even with all of your blessings and accomplishments, you are still holding on to the fact that you loved a horrible man. Now you fear that if you love again it will be wasted. But be encouraged that if you love again, it will be fulfilling. It can be and it will be if you will allow it." Aura stated soulfully.

I took a deep sigh and said, "It's not that I don't believe it can't happen again. Even with all of the prayers and accomplishments, I am still dealing with the keloided scar of depression. It's not sadness. It is the scars formed out of fears that were at one point rational."

Mai scooted closer to me and cupped my face, "Your soul is cleared of the spiritual filth, but that mind of yours still needs work. Cleansing is a process; you should not be ashamed of it. Come by tomorrow. I want to dig deeper into this."

I nodded and we turned our attention back to the celebration.

Mai had moved back into the city, which we were all surprised about because she loved the peace of the Hamptons. She kept the house open for our girl getaways or if she wanted to be left alone. Her place was on the upper east side of Manhattan where she had a clear view of the Hudson River and trees. I walked into her ornate modern building. When I got to her door I could hear her coughing vigorously. I knocked on the door. She welcomed me in while finishing a cough.

"Sis, you alright?" I asked.

"Yeah. I was drinking tea and it went down the wrong pipe." She laughed. "Do you want some tea? I ordered some Chinese food too if you're hungry.

I nodded and she fixed me some tea. We sat on the plush couch in her living room that was like a gallery view of New York City through her floor to ceiling windows. I sipped my tea and looked outside while I fixed my mouth to say what could've possibly broken Mai's heart. I took a deep breath and said,

"I suffer from depression."

Mai nodded, "I know, sis. It's not hard to spot. Tell me how you got this way."

I put my tea down and began "At the age of six, I was diagnosed with depression by a state appointed psychiatrist. To me though, it was more about being overwhelmed about the fact that I could not control how to fix my situation or the people around me."

I went on to explain that prior to being diagnosed with depression I remember sitting in the living room of a residential treatment center and always crying. The girls in my group home were all teenagers. Many days, I felt alone because I didn't have a relationship with any of them. I shared a room with a girl who often bullied me. Her bullying reminded me of the days I spent at home with my parents. I often had flashbacks of the ongoing abuse between my mother and father whenever they were around each other. Bullying became a part of my everyday life. Trying to deal with the harsh memories of abuse, being separated from my biological siblings and battling my own depression, kept me in a cluttered mental headspace.

All these things created a feeling of loss and emptiness, something that showed up again in my spiritual journey. My sleep patterns changed, I became uninterested in activities I loved such as track and field, and my (what type of behavior) behavior began to increase. If someone did something to me that made me uncomfortable, I would lash out by being rude and provoke them into physical altercations so that I had a reason to fight. Fighting gave me the adrenalin rush needed for me to release the tensions of life and the cards dealt to me. Fighting allowed me the opportunity to release the hurt, anger and rage being carried inside of me. My social worker spoke with the nurse at my agency and agreed that I needed to be seen by the agency psychiatrist again.

In less than a week, I was seen and the psychiatrist diagnosed me with clinical depression. According to the doctor, the symptoms being displayed was just the beginning of what was to come. Once diagnosed, counseling immediately began for me.

He recommended that I see a therapist on a weekly basis, start a low dose of Prozac and come to see him for regular monthly meetings.

"So, they took the time to see what was wrong with you after you hurt others and their reputation?" Mai asked, and I nodded, "Interesting what people will do for you when your problems start to affect them and not an instant before."

I continued, "I realized that the medication had a limit. It made me feel great and I could function around people, but then it would go away, and the demons nestled in me forced me to look at them through my reflection. I wanted to kill myself. I didn't want to bother anyone else and I also didn't want to be bothered. My first act of real courage in life was removing my medications. I wanted to work on me, but I was afraid to. Until I met you all."

Mai grinned and said, "And now all that is left is the heaven within."

"Yeah. But there was one day that I remember. It was the day someone stood up for me and I thought, *"someone finally cares."* You need that when you're a kid."

I was laying in the bed crying because my bully reminded me of the day I was laid out on the stretcher from a domestic altercation between my mother and father. I grabbed the pillow so tight and smashed my face into it while biting down on it with my clinching teeth. My head eventually lifted off of the bed and the pillowed was removed from my face. Sobbing with the salty tears and snot running down my face into my mouth I told my house mate *"She keeps on bullying me about how ugly I am. She teases me about not having any family to visit me and the way I dress. Am I that ugly that she can just treat me anyway she wants or is it because I am too small to defend myself?" No one else bothers me!"* My house mate grabbed my hand and marched me down the hallway dragging me while I almost fell flat on my face.

Soon as we reached the living room my housemate stood over the bully and told her to get up off the couch. The girl refused to get up and my house mate grabbed her by her hair pulling her up to her. "Leave her the fuck alone. The next time you decide to pick on someone, pick on me. Every day you continue to do something to her making her afraid of you. I'm not afraid of you and the next time I see her crying, or she tells me you're trying to punk her, I will whoop your ass for her." My house mate looked at me and shook her head. "You're ok now. If this happens again let me know. From that day forward, I never had another issue with the young lady that bullied me. Often, I would ask myself why she would bully someone so small and fragile. Maybe she was bullied and didn't know how to shake it by being kind to me by demonstrating the opposite of what she experienced.

"As time passed, I would seclude myself from people so my depression would not affect their life. After you all came along, I finally felt like I had many safe spaces and big sisters that would protect me from anything," I said tearfully.

"So why are you depressed now? You've been quite literally through a well of healing, life is looking up. I don't get it." Mai stated.

"Because although my soul is cleared, I have all these scars and I'm terrified that I will never love again. I don't think I have the capability to do it. There will always be a mental block."

Mai sighed and inched closer to me, "Mental illness caused by deeply rooted pain is like a relentless cancer. You do everything you can to get rid of it, manage it, and it will go away long enough to make you forget that it was there. Then it will rear its ugly head again and make you remember that it has a permanent space within you. The first time you come to know God and you recognize that the holy power has domain over everything. Then when it comes back you use it as fuel to make a difference. Perhaps, because you understand someone else's pain. The surprise is, when it comes back once more you realize you're running out of space to deal with it. And that you must submit to it because you're too tired. God's willing soldier has no more fight. And if you get to that point Sis, it's not your fault. You are a warrior with a task. So long as you finish your task nothing that takes you over can ever say it defeated you. You can feel this way...but FIGHT. If you don't fight against this, I'm going to be the big sister that kicks your ass." Mai began to sob.

I grabbed Mai up in a hug and said, "Mai. Mai what's wrong?"

"I-I-I..." Mai sobbed, "I have been battling different types of cancer since 2004. First it was ovarian and that is when my ancestor came to me and said, '*You have a task. You must reunite the war dogs and birth peace that my grandparents and parents never truly knew into their lives.*' Then I got lung cancer and God spoke to me saying that there are so many communities that cannot breathe. So, I used my money to create the foundation. Now, both are back and I asked God why. I pleaded with my ancestors, and some of yours petitioning for my healing. And they all said we know it hurts, but you can do far more from here than on earth. I am terrified although I know what is on the other side because I thought we could all live out this new life together. My brother told me about when he went to church with you and your uncle showed up. That message in the scripture…it wasn't for him; it was for me. I won't see that promised land with you, sis."

I wept and was scatterbrained trying to figure out how to fix this, "We-we can find alternative treatments there is always a way out. Come on! Come on! You gonna tell me to fight for my life but not fight for yours?! Come on!"

Mai began to dry her tears and said, "You still have a purpose to fulfill. I have done my part to help you fulfill it. My mother named me Mai, because it means coyote. And coyote's while tricky in their nature, are also a part of the incredible magic of creating a new life. I have lived up to my name. Now it is time for you to live up to your purpose. Fight this thing, Felicia. Dig deeper to use your soul to heal your mind."

∼

After Mai told me about her cancer all I could reflect on was how losing Beverly was what set off this chaos that became my life. What would losing Mai set off? I kept thinking about Beverly fighting for my soul. I somehow still felt disconnected from her. That disconnect resulted in mental health issues that arrested and kept me bound. When your mind is so scattered from past trauma it's hard to believe that water will wash it away. Mai reminded me that when you make yourself a clean slate it does not mean there is no debris left of the pain you've washed away. Scars are an honorable thing if you think about it. It is a reminder that you survived, but also a reminder to never go back to what caused the wound. Did that mean that I had to reject my mother? It was her absence that started me on this painful journey, yet it was also her love and my forgiveness that has brought me this far. I kept pacing around the living room racking my brain about how to move on.

I got lost in my pace around the living room. The window was slightly cracked open as the Harlem streets played me a tune over the autumn breeze. There were people yelling, honking horns, boisterous conversation, and children laughing. Jasmine made me love autumn in New York. The air smells like coffee, rain, nature, and cigars; it feels chilly enough to be cozy and warm enough to still enjoy the sites. It's a weird combination but your senses come to appreciate it and I loved to dance to the harmony of the streets and that air coming through the window. It made me forget my troubles and be present in my own spirit and the soul of the city.

Didi came and nudged me towards the couch to sit down. So, I complied as she nuzzled up next to me. I saw my prayer journal on the coffee table and picked it up. As I was about to start writing I heard a little girl yelling at her brother in front of the bodega across the street '*Mama told you have something sweet at home why are looking for more?!*' I chuckled and began writing in my journal:

You have something sweet at home why are you looking for more? I have found a new family that I always wanted. Having a connection with my ancestors has changed my perspective on life and spirituality completely. I feel the God in me, but yet I still feel so human. Things are finally starting to get on track, I think. I finally have the capacity to love and appreciate who I am, but I am still so troubled. I don't know what to do.

A strong wind blew in and crossed over all the mirrors in the living room touching each with a glimmer. Didi popped up and started barking, then suddenly the white candle on my ancestor altar fell over.

"Ok, who's here now? You're not popping up on me again, Pa!" I said jokingly. I kept looking around the room to see if I saw someone in a mirror. I got up and started walking towards my altar. "Auntie? Gran? Etta? Umm…"

I got close to my altar and looked in the mirror that sat above it and heard a whisper, "Pray for guidance." This spiritual world stuff continued to freak me out, but I had learned to listen. I sat down in front of my altar, picked up the candle, lit it, and started doing my deep breathing. I took one deep breath. And another. Then another and with that third release I felt the autumn wind surround me. Then I opened my eyes. I was standing in the middle of a circle in a sunflower field. It looked like a beautiful spring day with the sunflowers radiating their bright yellow and green, and calm winds passing through trees playfully shaking the leaves.

My admiration was interrupted by a startling, "Ahem!" I turned around and saw my mother sitting on the ground smiling with full fluffy curly hair down her back, bright eyes, and the sunlight dancing across her radiant skin and yellow haltered jumpsuit.

"I see you found the place." Beverly said with a smile.

Tears weld up in my eyes as I sat down in front of her and I said, "You look so beautiful Bev!"

She pulled her Ife cord from behind her back and swung it around by her knee and smirked, "Thank you, baby. I am finally a free spirit."

"What do you mean?" I asked.

"You forgave me which was part of setting me free. I had to forgive myself. Then had to learn about how to be a part of this world. No matter what stage in which we find ourselves in this endless life we have to learn to how to live in it. Now that I have learned how to be a part of the spirit, I am free." Beverly explained.

"So, is this your part of heaven? Like what Grandma Etta has?" I asked.

Beverly smiled and gently used her hands to clasp mine, "No, baby. We are within you. This is the heaven you have created inside."

My whole body quivered, and I started crying tears of joy that evolved into a laugh. Beverly laughed along with me and clapped as the birds around us started to chirp and the wind blew in celebration. I got up and danced around the circle to the music of my soul. I spun around my mother as she looked up at me with delight. When I finally plopped down to sit with her she laughed and hugged me tightly enough to where I felt like

I was within her again. She released me, gently took my hands and said,

"Come and take a walk with me, baby."

We got up, held hands, and walked through the vast sunflower field of my soul as the wind blew my mother's chiffon-like yellow jumpsuit making it danced across her radiant skin with her Ife cord draped and swaying behind her. As we gracefully walked through the sea of gold and green, I inquired why I had sunflowers within me. I could not understand why that would be when the sunflowers of Tribeland were put there by God and grown by spirit mothers and I was *not* a spirit mother and *certainly not God*, so what gives?

Bev erupted in a boisterous laugh like you hear from Black women sitting together for a joyous occasion, followed by a, '*whew child*' or '*girrrl*' with praise-like stomps and claps. She rocked her body around laughing, then hugged me and kissed my forehead. She took my hand again and we continued walking while I kept looking over at her with curious eyes waiting for her to explain. We approached another circle that was surrounded by different plots of land. I turned around looking at the different plots and saw that in one section some flowers were dying. In the next section, there was a vast area of undisturbed soil and some that had been toiled. And in the next some flowers that started to sprout. I looked back at Bev and threw my hands up with an inquisitive frustration.

Bev chuckled and explained, "Baby girl, you are absolutely right that you are not a spirit mother. You are, however, part of the spirit in an earthly form. Every sunflower that you see in full bloom are the tasks that you have completed to rise up to your better self. The great, the good, and the ugly. The plot we met in was your childhood all the way up to this point in time. They remain in bloom because they are complete and nourished by your determination to stay in peace and bloom for the rest of your life." She began to gracefully point to the different sections surrounding us and explained, "You see these dying flowers? They no longer serve a purpose in your growth, nor are they nourished by your peace. It was the toxicity that kept them alive; however, the seeds from those lessons and experiences will drop down and replant themselves to remind you of your strength which will keep you grounded through other tasks. God don't waste no souls, and don't waste their seeds neither. This will happen time and time again throughout your life. When your soul ascends to be with us so shall this garden be released back to the Most High, like the spirits grown in Tribeland, so they can be used as nourishment for next set of souls being raised."

"So where is your garden?" I asked.

Bev cupped my face lovingly and said, "Only a few of my flowers bloomed but never replanted to be able to grow a vast harvest such as this. I could not move on from the pain of losing my mother, then my father, then my sense of self. I suffered loss after loss and never found my way back to a peaceful place. My flowers held their weight in water, but it only generated one hopeful seed, you."

"I just don't get it. Auntie Eva is still mad about stuff, still sad about things, anything that could possibly put her back in the well or on the horse. And she's living the life in heaven!" I stated.

Bev released my face and grabbed my hand to invite me to the ground and sit with her. "You can be mad or sad about something while you are also at peace with it. It's on your soul's memory like a scar, but it doesn't have to hurt forever...it's just there. When I died, I was stuck in that well because I never found peace with the anguish of what I had done. I begged to get off the horse and out of that well, but Ife said, 'Our baby needs to forgive you and you need to forgive yourself for leaning into the curses on our bloodline and accepting it as truth instead of fighting against it.'" She took a deep quivering breath and continued, "This has been a hard journey for you. Even though I couldn't see it, I could feel it within my being and was only able to reach you through your dreams to warn you not to be like me. But I was not strong enough to speak. However, it took both of us to accept my failure to grow and do better, that set us both free. I'm grateful for your hardships that made you a fighter because every tear, every revelation, every pain inflicted on you has turned you into this," She stretched out her arms swiveled her body around showing off my garden.

Without any hesitation I jumped into my Mother's arms, knocking her over, and we rolled around on the ground getting twisted up in her Ife cord. We laughed and cried as I thought back to seeing her in that well. Living through what felt like pure hell and still being able to grow my garden. God don't waste no souls, as Auntie Eva says, we end up right where we are supposed to be. My Mother's life may have looked like a waste, but she planted her seed allowed it to grow past her own capacities. Even from a place beyond the stars she fought for my life and when she had the strength, she spoke power into my soul. I had a mother this whole time.

I felt like I had become my ancestors' dream. I conquered the odds, cleared out curses, and even though I was battling depression and anxiety it was a mesh barrier between who I am now and who I will be. Nothing was going to stop me. I had plans to execute! It was time to bring honor to the family name and it was going to start with me! My ancestors paid on the blood curses, but now I am settling the debts! It was time to uproot and replant to bring joy back into the bloodline.

My mother released me, and we collected ourselves and stood up. She took a deep breath, closed her eyes, turned her palms upward and began to hum the tune that the spirit mothers sing to release the new souls. Her Ife cord began to glow and suddenly there was a flash of yellow and white neon light. Then a book from the library in Tribleand appeared. She reminded me that these books are for whispering ideas into the souls and minds of descendants to motivate, inspire, or change their course. They whisper it in a divine language that is a mirror reflection of what it means in the human language. I remembered that Mai and Aura told me this is why they must reflect on a living being to speak the human language because now all they speak is the divine language of God.

"When you hear that quiet voice or have a sudden thought that was not within the realm of what you were originally thinking, that's us speaking to you. Whether it is commanded by God or our own divine wisdom we get the message to you so you can do what you need to do."

"Well why do you have it now? I'm standing right here. You can tell me in plain English," I said.

"We are within you, remember? I will speak this to your soul as you return to your body. You will understand the message when you awaken from your meditation. I love you, Sunshine. I'll be right here if you need me," my mother said with a gleaming smile and love twinkling in her eyes.

She began speaking the divine language that sounded like whispers in a hurricane with the accent of my Nigerian ancestors. "*Smaerd tsedliw srotsecna rou ton rea uoy.*"

I was pulled backwards by a forceful wind as the sunflowers faded away and I floated backwards towards a bright light hearing the words of my mother that sounded like gibberish. The closer I got to the light the more it translated.

"Smaerd tsedliw srotsecna rou ton rea uoy.

You are not our ancestors' wildest dreams." (You are? Or You are not as written her?)

They never could have imagined a being such as yourself. You are the collection of many dreams, hopes, fears, and strengths strung together into one powerful seed. From that one seed will grow a garden of hope and create an impact that the world has never seen.

"Smaerd tsedliw srotsecna rou ton rea uoy

You are not our ancestors' wildest dreams."

You are their greatest hope to complete the task that we could not, to be the warrior that can withstand the burn of battles and win the war against the bloodline and triumph over the curses on our souls. Sweet child, I am not your answer, I am your guide. You are the answer

and give life to the collective dream, to align and manifest the souls'
prosperity. Do not worry yourself with the toils of days ahead. You
have everything you need to grow your garden and be at peace."

My eyes shot open. I was sweating so profusely that there was a small puddle surrounding me. I sat trying to catch my breath and eventually collapsed on the floor and stared at the ceiling. The autumn Harlem wind blew through the door once more and I smiled thinking about the message. Mama Christina burst through the door and started yelling, "*Felicia! Mija, if you're sleeping wake up, we're going to get tostones!*" I couldn't move. I laid on the floor smiling as I realized that all of this was to prepare me for creating a new bloodline through the seeds sown for all-around prosperity. I am not my illness; I am a sunflower woman.

EBB & FLOW

〜〜〜・〜〜〜

"Challenges are what make life interesting; overcoming them is
what makes life meaningful."
– Joshua J. Marine

I WAS NERVOUS about losing Mai. She had fought so hard
for all of us to be together as sisters and suffered in silence so
we could bloom into our best selves. Mick was distraught and
cussing out every doctor he could, saying that he paid an obscene
amount of money to make sure this did not happen. But the fact
is with cancer, it is indiscriminatory, much like any other illness.

I decided to finally take her advice and be open to love. Right
when I made that decision I was leaving from school and got a
text from Jasmine saying she wanted me to meet a man named
Troy who also worked in child welfare and wanted to give an
inside look at what I might be up against. One meeting turned
into another and another meeting turned into a date. Then those
dates turned into *us* dating.

This was happening so fast that I did not trust it. So, I went
to God on it. I asked God and my ancestors if I should jump in
and take a chance on this love. I heard nothing, saw nothing,
and believed that this was a fluke and would go on its way. After
being romanced then abused by Reggie I couldn't trust Troy and
didn't want to. I told him to his face one day,

"You are going to disappoint me like any other man, and I
am honestly counting the days."

He looked at me, held me close, then said in the most soothing voice, "There will be times that I may disappoint you, but I will never be a disappointment. I love you and will always seek for you to live in this love with me as we grow as people, a couple, and prayerfully one day a family."

I was so stunned. There was nothing for me to say. I ran to the hospital where Mai was and told her about my prayer and what he said. She took off her oxygen mask, climbed out of bed, put her hands on her hips and said, "Well you got your answer, didn't you?!"

We both laughed and she continued, "When is the wedding?"

Marriage had never crossed my mind, especially after Reggie. Low and behold, he proposed two weeks later, and we eloped!

After Troy and I eloped, the next few weeks were a whirlwind of visiting Mai in the hospital, keeping up with school, and settling into my new life. Cara and Prism were thriving with their healing center, and Aura's spiritual practice was getting stronger every day. She would visit Mai in the hospital often to laugh with her and petition the ancestors to save her; even though she felt it was futile.

One morning I felt...off. My husband was doing well, I was well overall, but something just felt off. I tried to get my day started by checking my planner and organizing my papers. Then when I looked at the date, I realized I missed my period. *"Oh shit."* I thought. As soon as it hit me, I got incredibly nauseous and ran to the bathroom and started throwing up. My husband was startled from his sleep and ran towards the bathroom after first running into the wall.

"Felicia! Baby, what is wrong! You sick? You got the flu or something?" Troy asked.

"Not a flu...a baby." I said with my head in the toilet.

"A baby what? A human baby?!" Troy said in dumbfounding confusion

I sat up from the toilet and shouted, "No honey an ocelot! YES, a human baby!"

"We're having a baby?! Oh my God! Really! I...I'm going to be a daddy?!"

He swooped me up in his arms and carried me back to bed and would not stop celebrating! We went to the doctor to make sure that everything was alright, and they raised an eyebrow looking at my bloodwork. They told me to visit a genetics counselor.

When I met with the genetics counselor, she asked me questions that I was never asked before. In my mind I thought why does she need all of this information for?

First question asked was "is there anyone in your family with down syndrome or intellectual disabilities or neurological issues?"

Looking at her, I immediately answered no. Then she asked what about heart problems or any known diseases?"

I responded yes. Blood pressure. But little did I know there were more underlying issues brewing underneath the rug. Eight months and grueling birth later, our son Jabez was born, and I noticed a liquid filled sack on the lower part of his spine. Immediately, I knew something was wrong. Every time his father and I sat him up on a pillow, he would fall right over not even able to push or try to push himself up like most babies.

I called the pediatric doctor and she told us to bring him in immediately. When we arrived at the doctor's office the following week and she examined him the look on her face told it all.

"Well mom and dad, he will need to see a Neurologist. He has fluid leaking from his spine. What he has is called Spina Bifida".

In my mind all I can think of was what did I do wrong during my pregnancy? We got the "script" to see the specialist at the children's hospital and took him in. When we first met the neurologist, he let me and my husband know that we made it to him right on time. Jabez saw him one time when he was just a month old and stated that he will have to go into surgery at three months old to avoid paralysis from the waist down. According to the Neurologist, "He will need this surgery without a question because if he doesn't get the surgery, he will not be able to walk at all, and will be in a wheelchair by the time he turns one." I was not a doctor, but I knew that if we didn't proceed, he wouldn't stand a chance at a normal life.

My Sunflower family surrounded me, including Mai who was clinging to life in a wheelchair, so that they could be there for me at the hospital when Jabez had his surgery. My husband and I didn't leave the hospital until the neurologist came out into the waiting room to inform us of how the surgery went.

While waiting, all I could do was pray and ask God to bless the surgeon's hand and keep my son covered.

As the surgeon came through the secured doors, I immediately jumped up and walked over to him. Without saying a word, he looked at me and said "Jabez is going to be okay. He has a great chance of walking and being able to move his lower legs. He is in the ICU unit and will be there for at least three to five days so that he can be observed, and his nerves monitored. He will remain there until we feel confident enough to send him home".

The relief that came over me was everything I needed in that moment. I slept in the hospital every day. My husband and I would rotate so that we could both get some rest. I stayed during the night and he stayed during the day so I could go home and get myself together. The day Jabez was cleared to go home came with a lot of responsibilities for his physical development. Because he was just three months old when he had his surgery he had to be monitored closely for any changes. One of the visible changes we noticed right away was that he could not move his legs a lot following surgery. With the muscle spasms taking place, that was the only time he would kick and try to lift his legs up. Outside of that, he would rest them on the mattress. This continued for about a week.

Once home, I would rub his legs and lift them up and down to give him some exercise and encourage him to move his legs on his own. After a few rubs and movement, he began doing it on his own. Then by the time he was six months old he was out of the danger zone and cleared by the doctor to have no nerve damage. Moving forward, Jabez began crawling and standing with no problem. With everything moving along, I began to shift gears as a parent and move in the direction of normalcy. Jabez started going to daycare, where he did extremely well.

I called Mai at home where she was receiving hospice care and told her the wonderful news about how well Jabez was doing. Through her weakened state she cried tears of joy and said she knew everything would be alright. Then she said, "Don't worry, I know there is something wonderful coming because something wonderful has already happened. Jump into that hope sis; it can take you so far."

A week later Mick was banging on my door and when I ran to open it, he was on his knees sobbing and I knew. I called the rest of our family; there was a haunting silence that I had never heard before. They knew she was with our ancestors, but it also meant that we could not hug her here. We gathered for the funeral at her house and sat out by the lake. She had requested a small ceremony because she did not want a big fuss. Mick stood up in his bright blue suit and tired red eyes and said,

"My sister asked me to read this letter at her funeral, because a eulogy would not suit her when she simply wanted to get to the point. She already knows the life that she has lived and so do the people who are present here today:

"Life is a journey, and the destination is not death. Some see death as the end, but it is indeed a climax because we don't know what's next. While on the side that we understand, make your life count by jumping into whatever pool of new adventures present itself. This is not easy, this whole ride. But damn...what a ride it is, and it is well. Run fast, eat everything, and love all as I love you. Jump in. Farewell."

HOLDING WATER // FELICIA R. WILSON

APHULE

~~~~. ~~~~

"You don't make progress by standing on the sidelines,
whimpering, and complaining. You make progress by
implementing ideas"
– Shirley Chisholm

THE LAST FEW years had brought me full circle to exactly
what I wanted. I marinated on the lessons, love, and experiences
that I had with my Sunflower family. It was time for me to
put this all into action. It was never going to be perfect. I had
experience, a plan, a dream, and it was all coming from my soul.
But was it enough?

As I was finishing up my degree, I didn't know whether my
work would be with youth in the criminal justice system or in
foster care. While working for the New York City Department
of Juvenile Justice, I would see more and more foster youth
entering the system. Often, I thought, *why is this happening?* The
reality of it was due to agencies not having foster homes to place
teenagers. Some of the youth that walked through the detention
doors didn't fit in like some of the youth that were out there
getting themselves mixed up and being accused of breaking the
law. Once more I went down a rabbit hole of thoughts about how
things could change, how I could I walk in my purpose and not
my pride?

When I learned from one of the youths that they ended up
in detention for following their peers and engaging in negative

behavior and activities, I knew that something needed to change. As a youth growing up in foster care, finding foster homes to place youth in was extremely difficult. More so, it was due to foster parents having the wrong perception of teenagers. Teenagers in foster care were, and are often looked at as problematic youth. But, in all reality, all they needed was someone to show them love, support and understand that they want to feel a part of a loving family. They needed someone to let them know that they were not dogs, but gods.

As a child I would often hear foster parents talking amongst each other about how foster children were latchkey kids, emotionally disturbed and deemed to fail in society. Remembering these things being said continued to stick with me over the years. To be honest, the negative things often said gave me strength to prove many foster parents wrong. One of the things that troubled me the most was that many foster parents always wanted babies and school-aged children. What they didn't realize at the time of making their request for younger children was that even younger children become teenagers.

I can recall the day that I was leaving one foster home and going into another one. The foster mother's home in which I was living called the foster home I was going to and began telling my new foster mother how horrible I was, and not to take me. This crushed my heart. I was a teenager acting out because I just wanted to feel like I was a part of a family that accepted me for my flaws, good, bad, and indifferent. All I ever wanted was to know that someone had my back and would fight for me just like they would do for their children. Growing up in the foster care system made me bitter. But after looking at the circumstances and odds stacked against me, I decided to take a stand and advocate for what was right. The first thing I did was begin advocating for myself. Doing so, allowed me to see what areas of my own life needed improvement and force the hands of those responsible for me to do their job and what was in my best interest.

I went directly to my law guardian and the social worker under her with anything I wanted done that my foster parents and case workers refused to do. If things were aligned and made sense and contributed to my growth moving forward my law guardian and her team was onboard to advocate for me and what the agency needed to do to ensure that things get done. Having a legal representative appointed by the family court to represent me and any foster child limits what the foster parents and agency can do when it comes to the child. With the support of my family court judge and legal system, I decided to use my rights as a means to force my agency and tie their hands when it came to them telling me what was going to happen for me.

Instead, what I did was use the Foster Child Rights Guidebook that was given to me by my law guardian to advocate better for myself. This guidebook informed me of everything that I was entitled to and covered everything from giving my own ten-day notice to be moved, visits with siblings and other family members, phone calls, clothing and even allowance to name a few. The guidebook was the beginning of what I needed to help ensure that my basic rights were being met. I began seeing an ongoing trend of teenagers being hard to place and detention being used as an alternative. That sparked the advocate in me.

Change started by first finding out what services were missing when I was in care. One of the things that stood out to me was the need to prepare youth aging out of foster care into adulthood. In addition, I realized that in order for youth to successfully, transition into the adult world certain services needed to be in place - to personal development, professional development and independent living services. These services would provide the necessary tools to further assist them, and provide a foundation for moving forward in life. Knowing that these areas are often lacking in youth, I took a stand to implement programs that would benefit and help them excel across the board.

I knew from my own experience how much I benefited from this type of support. Implementing a system from a foster care alumnus viewpoint would, and could engage youth in foster care better. When I was in the process of aging out of the child welfare system, case managers were coming and going as if they were on a roller coaster. Often, I thought of why this was happening. One of the things I came to realize was that there was a lack of leadership from administration such as directors and supervisors, case workers, and socio-therapists..

Many times, the worker would ask me questions that they should have already known if they read my records. Clearly, the questions asked was a dead giveaway that they were uninterested about the youth they were assigned to help. Experiencing things like a high turnover rate in case workers, nurses and ACS workers demonstrated to youth in foster care that they were viewed as disposable. Having to meet a new worker every ninety days became more and more traumatizing as the seconds, minutes, days, and months went on. There were plenty of days I thought about what it would feel like to have someone that was consistent in my life that offered ongoing and lasting support.

What most do not realize is that no one knows or can dictate how a child will turn out. This includes your biological child, foster child, or any child being raised by a responsible. Remembering the many challenges I faced with trusting those making decisions for me, I vowed to be the change in the world to help foster children achieve in life and into adulthood.

First, there were some steps that I needed to put in place. I had to put myself in a position to help the public understand what happens within the troubled walls of the foster care system. Often, people only see or hear one side of the story. Usually, the negative side of how bad, disrespectful, and defiant teenagers in foster care are. See, many people in society seem not to understand that applying names to children often damages their self-esteem, tears down their character, and labels them before they are ever given an opportunity to show up in the world.

As for myself, I learned to fight the stigmas attached by educating the public and anyone that didn't understand exactly what foster care is about. Being able to maneuver around the uncomfortable questions of my life as a child made it less complicated for me to listen and hear as I grew into my teenage years. Hearing the word foster child started to sink in. As a child in the system, foster care was publicized but not to the extent to which it is today. Raising awareness of the needs of youth regarding their mental health, educational stability is critical as is the importance of a transitional plan for those aging out of the system. The ages of 18 – 21 for foster children is crucial. This was it, I had everything I needed to make the changes that were necessary... or so I thought.

I wanted to create a platform for them to breathe and voice their concerns. Speaking on platforms for adoption and foster care gave me the courage to be as loud as Mick, bold as Cara, vulnerable as Aura, healing a Prism, and as wise as Mai. As I became more connected with administrators, alumni of foster care and adoptees from all over the world, I began to learn from them that they felt the same way I did. Like me, they too saw that children and youth leaving the system had needs that were not being met. Teenagers aging out of the system with little to no safety net in place struggled to support themselves. It was even more difficult for foster children who had children of their own. Most times, they were discharged to homeless shelters where they hoped to quickly receive housing assistance. Receive.

No networks or supports in place mean no sense of permanence or stability of those teenagers that have reached or nearing the age of 18. The only sure thing they can do is legally make the independent decision to leave or stay in foster care. Knowing this, I encourage them to stay until they are 21 years of age. This provides more time for them to receive services designed to support and help them start the process of transitioning. The goal is help them start with the necessary tools for successful, independent living. Youth with a goal of independent living must start the process at least five to seven years prior so that they have all supports and services lined up to start the transition process. Those who reach the age of 21 are usually are not ready to step out on their own. Agencies responsible for youth prior to them aging out must extend services until the age of twenty-five. By the time they reach age twenty-five, youth in foster care should be able to handle adulthood and maintain themselves with services in place to assist them if they need additional support.

I figured that one of the best ways to implement an effective approach is to include the foster youth and get their take on what they want and would like to see happen. Next, agencies should start the process to move them in the right direction by the time they reach the age of fourteen by notifying the social worker that the child is not interested in permanency/adoption. Starting youth on the road to independence as early as possible is key. It gives them the structure, discipline and resources to be successful beyond child welfare services. Advocating for the youth in foster care has often been dismissed and put on the back burner for so long that children continue to fall through the cracks ending up in poverty, facing homelessness and even dealing with incarceration as it provides them with an alternative to having shelter over their heads and off the street. Implementing change came with a price for me.

The price is about vulnerability and allowing myself to put my life on the forefront for the youth that don't know which way to go and what to do. Allowing myself to be vulnerable gave me the power of my own self-control while being unapologetically me. Now, it's about stepping into the light so that foster youth can get everything they have been deprived of. Implementing change needed to start with me first. I needed to face the obstacles of my own downfall in order to see what I would stand for. Knowing how to help Felicia, I am able and capable of advocating for the youth that have no one to come to their defense and rescue them.

As I paced around the living room and jumped back and forth to my desk writing these ideas and envisioning them, I realized that I was the answer to my own prayers that I had for someone to rescue me. Yet somehow, I still felt like that little girl who needed to be coddled and raised. Here I was a mother trying to save my own son from what was surely going to be a detriment to his life, and yet I was still trying to save my own. I washed away the soul ties that were ripping me from a greater destiny, but I could not grapple with the scars they left behind.

RIVERS

ᨁᨁᨁ . ᨁᨁᨁ

I KEPT PACING until I collapsed on the couch and drifted off into sleep. I stirred when I thought I heard the baby about to wake up, but it was just my husband rolling over and talking in his sleep. I took a deep sigh and nestled myself into the couch wrapped in Mai's blanket. I awakened laying on a shoreline after what felt like a full night's sleep. I was surrounded by a jungle with trees and flower filled bushes that were iridescent then in full bloom and then changing colors. It was as if the plants were trying on different outfits for their day ahead. I knew I was in the spirit world, but this was not Tribeland, this was...different. Suddenly I heard a melodic howl in the distance.

'AAAYOOOO'

I jumped up and frantically looked left and right for the animal. Finally, I turned towards the ocean, and there standing three feet away from me with waves washing across her feet stood Mai. She opened her arms elegantly, showing off her white sleeves and red dress that twinkled in the sun. I ran towards her and leapt into her arms in tears, grasping onto her spirit never wanting to let go. She pulled back from me and caressed my arms then said,

"For the record, you're not dead."

We both laughed and I asked, "So where am I now?"

"I have been given a final task, to bring you to the source of your soul line," Mai explained.

"I miss you so much. Can I come see you whenever I want? We still need you," I begged.

"I'll show up if you really need me. I've come to find that the answers we seek are usually within. That's my cornball way of saying, you got this sis!" Mai laughed.

"Are you ok? You didn't get stuck on the horse, did you?" I asked.

"Not for too long. I was there because I missed you all. But I had to let you all go and take my place here. I don't love you any less, but my task was done and yours is still on going. There is so much for you to see sis, in your world and this one."

"What am I going to do with my son? This new life? My new purpose? This illness? I...I thought I finally had it together and then this sh-"

"Sis! Jump in. It's never going to be perfect and probably won't always feel right. But if you have the courage to jump in, you will land in the miracle that is the lesson or the blessing. Don't stop the possibility of your miracles. It is truly all we have." Mai caressed my face as she said this.

She kissed my cheek, hooked my arm and walked me into the fluorescent jungle. We passed by flowers that changed from white lilies to blue roses and finally glowing iridescent sunflowers. We came upon a village where I saw African women weaving baskets draped in clothing that was both ancient and somehow current in their twisted dresses ordained in jewels and patterns. I saw children molding clay pots and jars from the red soil that danced across my bare feet, dressed in vibrant shirts and dresses that twinkled on their skin as the sun did the clay. They all sat in front of their varying clay doorways and cheerily glanced at as I passed by, then continued working on their projects. A woman in a yellow dress with butterfly sleeves smiled at me and waved. Another woman in a purple gown that flowed with the wind blew a kiss at me and waved. A little boy darted from his doorway somehow not getting any red dirt on his all white outfit and ran towards me smiling with his arms open.

I bent down and caught him in my arms as he hugged me tightly and said, "I knew you'd make it here. They're waiting for you, come on."

Mai released my arm as the boy pulled me away and shouted, "Sis! Stop, Drop…"

"Shut 'em down open up shop! Oh, no, that's how rough riders roll!" We shouted in unison

We gleamed at each other and she faded away back into the jungle.

He pulled me along as he ran towards four women standing in the miraged distance. The first woman was dressed in a blue jeweled dress that was wrapped across her chest and over her shoulder. As she moved closer towards me, I saw the illuminated cord and realized it was Beverly.

"I see you finally made it here baby. I know you're probably wondering where you are." Beverly said

"I thought that this was Tribeland but honestly I'm not sure where I am," I said.

"Do you remember that Eva said that heaven is a vast space?" Beverly asked. I nodded and she continued, "Well this is also a part of it. You see we use Tribeland to communicate to the other side, baptize souls, and raise new souls. But this is also a place where we can rest and sow our own wishes for our bloodline. The women that are making baskets have thought about every strand that has gone into that basket; those are the new families, prayers for prosperity, and breaking curses. Sometimes our prayers are answered by the very people we wished them for, other times they go unanswered because the same people make different choices. Yet we are here all the way. I made terrible choices that made my garden barren, but Ife still wove my name to bear someone that would break our curse. That prayer went to the creator and the creator made the seed. You were raised by Eva and the spirit mothers of the women you call sisters. The women weaving baskets smile at you because they know you are here to take part in weaving a new basket."

"But I'm a human. I don't have the power to weave anything." I stated solemnly.

Suddenly, a woman with mocha skin and bright eyes wearing an orange medieval African style dress that was adorned in blue jewels gracefully sashayed towards us with a smile that was as bright as the jungle flower crown woven into her long curly hair. She took my hands, pulled me into a hug and said,

"Welcome home baby. I'm Ife."

I pulled back in shock and said, "Ife? Like Ife, Ife? The original?"

She chuckled and playfully opened her arms revealing all the cords connected to her from under her gown. The cords stretched out all around her and collected themselves together from her womb. I jumped away and fumbled around trying not to step on anyone's cords. Ife laughed and closed her arms which made the cords invisible again.

"Yes baby, that Ife. You call me grandma; we're going to have a problem." She said as we both laughed. She linked up to my arm and we began walking through the village. "I am the beginning of the bloodline that you have come to know through all the women you've met. When I was born, my task was to start a new bloodline. The old had been tarnished with their own issues and antics. Unfortunately, in some parts of the bloodline that became true for me too."

"Are you angry about that?" I asked.

"Yes and no. No one wants someone they love to suffer. I have found that God has a way of testing our strengths through strife. I know you must be wondering what's the point of all the suffering; if the strife, the struggles, the pain, the joys, the innovations - if it's all meaningless in the end. I tell you no it is not."

We walked towards a river that had white and luminescent stones on the riverbank. Ife led me to gently sit down on the rocks by the riverside. She picked up a blue rock and tossed it into the river making it come to a halt mid-stream. I giggled in amazement and Ife smiled, took a breath and said,

"You were anointed for a hefty task, beloved, just as I was. The components were all there to make you a mother of a new bloodline. You were connected to this path through key players that forced you to look inward and attach yourself to your power."

The stilled water rose up and formed into a mirror like screen. Ife went on to explain that in order to prepare me for my purpose there were different things I needed. She showed me when I left out of the child welfare office and my grandfather sang, *'If you want to be strong, challenge a dog. If you want to be invincible, challenge a god. Challenge your god! You ain't no dog you a god, you a god!'* It was a signal for me to start my journey. It was up to me to decide whether or not I was going to make changes. Then one by one, she explained that I needed some honesty and the screen showed Etta, Bobby, and Cara. Next, she told me that I needed some faith and showed me Illeri, Trey, Uncle Charles, and Aura. Ife continued explaining as visions of people in my life displayed. She stated that Mai and Eva were my path to wisdom, Jasmine was my encouragement, Reggie and Mick were my enlightenment, my husband taught me trust, and my mother taught me courage and forgiveness.

Ife tossed a black stone at the screen and it collapsed back into the river than began to run again. She took me by the hands and said, "You have had and will continue to have everything you need to become worthy enough to start a new bloodline."

"Ife, I've already started a bloodline and its falling apart already. I have two children. One who has spina bifida and the other…"

"Greeted you when you entered the village. While he was in your womb, he was never meant to be yours. His soul was released and here it waits to be joined with his true mother. Even still, he remembers you and looks after your boy." Ife explained.

I began to sob, "That was him?! I am still so lost, Ife! How am I supposed to be worthy of starting a new bloodline if I can't even get myself straight? I went through all of that to end up back here feeling lost and worthless!"

Ife yanked me closer to her in anger, then took a breath, smirked and said, "Every drop of water holds its own weight in the ocean. It seems so insignificant as it rolls through the waves, but without it, the waves would not move the same. So, what makes you think, little seed, that the water you hold is not significant when it can change the current of your life and the lives of others?"

My sob was silenced. I was stunned by what she said. Was I making myself feel insignificant? Did I suffer the way I had so future generations will not suffer? Am I indeed a god of my own world? Before I could ask her any of this she said,

"Your roots run deep, traumatized as they may be, yet you bloom and yield something new over and over again. You will never stop blooming. Hold on to your water, baby, and ride the wave while you chase the sun until it is your turn to come ashore and be with us here to raise more fields of future glory."

"What do I do now Ife?" I asked.

She pierced my soul with her strong and loving eyes and without moving her lips I heard her echoing whisper say, 'Plant your seeds and grow your field.'.

∾

I woke up to Jabez fretting and wanting to be held. I picked him up and walked to a window looking out at a city that no one could ignore. Remembering that I broke the ground for new gardens of opportunity to grow. My hieroglyphics were still being painted because I was a living word of God with every step and breath I took. The souls that made me were louder than any curse that could defeat me and will carry me as I walk in my purpose and my pain that will shape me. I am a city, I am a miracle, I hold my weight in the oceans of this world, I am alive.

It is well.

ABOUT THE AUTHOR

FELICIA WILSON WAS born in the Bronx, New York and was raised between Queens and Wyandanch, New York. She is the CEO and Founder of Fear Everything and Rise, LLC. Felicia works primarily with foster care youth ages 16+: those who need to prepare to age out, those that have aged out, and even those that have found themselves in the criminal justice system. Her mission is to empower young people and those that aged out of foster care the opportunity to be heard by speaking their pain and challenging themselves to overcome their circumstances. In 1984, Felicia began her journey through the New York City foster care system, where she spent the next seventeen years of her life moving from home to home.

Suffice to say, it was not an easy road. One of the many lessons Felicia learned while in the foster care system was, no matter what her past circumstances were she could rise above them. She realized she had the right to choose and control her own destiny. So she has dedicated her life to giving back and helping other foster care children so they won't have to travel some of the same dark paths she did.

Felicia now teaches young people to understand their past and present situation is not a precursor for the rest of their lives, but a prerequisite to the greatness they will share with the rest of the world. She believes, given the right tools and strategies, these young people can blossom into mature women and men, making their own impact in the world while changing one life at a time.

Felicia was Dean Listed at John Jay College of Criminal Justice in Manhattan New York where she studied Criminal Justice and specialized in Government. She finished her undergraduate studies at the University of Phoenix where she received her Bachelor of Science degree in Criminal Justice Administration. She then furthered her education at Walden University where she studied Human and Social Services and graduated with her Master of Science Degree in 2018. Currently Felicia is working on her Doctorate of Public Administration degree with Walden University.

Felicia spent 8 ½ years working for the New York City Department of Juvenile Justice and the New York City Administration for Children Services, where she served under the New York City Division of Youth and Family Justice. She also worked as a Congregate Care Specialist working in a residential setting with at risk youth that were awaiting sentencing for crimes such as rape, robbery, arson and violation of probation just to name a few.

Felicia remains dedicated to nurturing young people and helping them find their purpose in the world. She empowers them to be world leaders by implementing social change starting with themselves. She teaches the importance of community engagement, especially dealing with matters very close to them. When faced with challenges she is willing to challenge herself and learn from them. Felicia leads by example. She is a woman who perseveres and keeps pushing towards her dreams. Giving up is not an option as she continues to remember what's most important in life: her family.

www.ingramcontent.com/pod-product-compliance
Lightning Source LLC
Chambersburg PA
CBHW060020100426
42740CB00010B/1539